My Weekly Work

THE 28-WEEK MEMORY WORK

COMPANION JOURNAL

by Amy Atkins

USING THIS NOTEBOOK
ON CHRIST THE SOLID ROCK WE STAND

This student notebook is a blank canvas for all of your memory work through the weeks ahead no matter what curriculum you use.

It is designed as a companion to go along with your family's curriculum. Here you can write your facts, memory work, and more all in one place to file away and remember as your child progresses. All you need is a pencil and paper and this makes it easy for you.

Learn. Grow. Abide.

HOW TO USE EACH SECTION IN THIS NOTEBOOK

JOURNAL PAGE: This is to be used for things that start of your week. Jot down thoughts, goals, stories, prayer requests, interesting facts from a documentary, or other day-starting reflections.

WEEKLY OVERVIEW: At the begining of the week, write in your general topic for the week. You can include book titles or anything that you will be doing on your own at home. Math and Language Arts are more personal, individual choices and can be added in. Make it simple for younger students. Eventually, you will pass this essential skill of "planning" along to your growing student as they enter more challenging years.

HISTORY: Copy down your history sentence here. There is a place to write it 1-3 times. The blank open space is where you can draw it out, script free-hand, or paste a picture of the event.

GEOGRAPHY: Locate and label your weekly geography the best you can on this generic world map. If you need to draw a close-up view, draw or trace it on a separate paper and tape it in (prevent glue wrinkles). Use color pencils to make the select locations come alive on this black and white template.

TIMELINE: Create a timeline from your weekly memory work list. You make also choose to purchase our separate Timeline Journal to keep everything you learn together in one family book.

MATH: Create your own table, game, maze, and more! Simply write it out or make it fun.

SCIENCE: Write in your science memory facts and write a little bit about it as you learn and research.

BIBLE: Whether you are learning a hymn or Bible verse, write in the parts of the passage here. Below, answer the generic questions to apply this to our lives.

LATIN: Copy down the Latin for the week in this section. Write the previous week in from memory.

ENGLISH: Just like Latin, copy the memory work, write a story, or get creative with how you want to review.

EXAMPLE PAGES

WEEK ONE

WRITE IN A GENERAL OVERVIEW OF YOUR WEEKLY MEMORY WORK TO GIVE YOURSELF A WEEKLY AT-A-GLANCE OF YOUR WEEK AHEAD.

 **HISTORY
TIMELINE
GEOGRAPHY**

In 410, Barbarians invaded, Rome burned...

Continents and Oceans

Creation, Fall in the Garden...

ENGLISH

8 Parts of Speech

Subject-Verb agreement

HOW TO USE THE MAPS

These maps of course are not directly from your curriculum but it is important that children learn how to spot their geogrpahy no matter what map is presented to them. Here's how they can customize their maps:

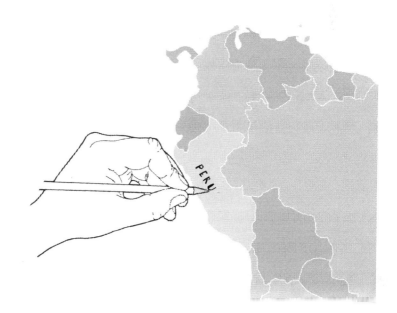

EXAMPLE PAGES

WEEKLY TIMELINE

Label the year(s) and write the event in order from earliest (top) to latest (bottom).

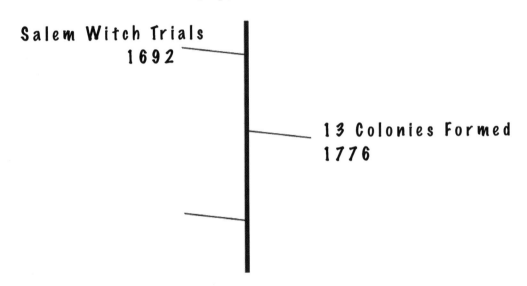

Salem Witch Trials
1692

13 Colonies Formed
1776

Write a sentence or short story that includes some of the memory work as an example.
Or, diagram a sentence or two.

My cat ate his food.

Cat - noun

ate - verb

My - adjective

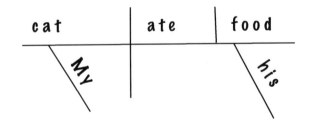

EXAMPLE PAGES

MATH

WEEK 1

Copy your math memory work here:

1, 2, 3, 4, 5, 6, 7, 8, 9, 10, 11, 12

2, 4, 6, 8, 10, 12, 14, 16, 18, 20, 22, 24

3, 6, 9, 12, 15, 18, 21, 27, 30, 33, 36

Make your own math problems and solve them:

1 x 2 = 2

3 x 3 = 9

3 x 8 = 24

Make your own number math maze, game, or
simply copy the memory work again:

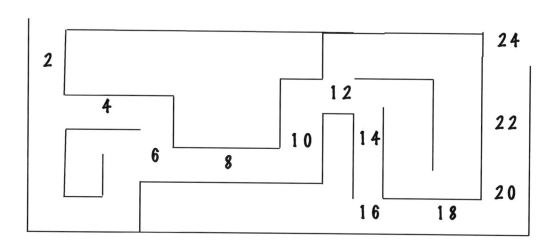

JOURNAL

HERİTAGE

Week 1

"IT IS MY PRAYER THAT YOUR LOVE MAY ABOUND MORE AND MORE, WITH KNOWLEDGE AND ALL DISCERNMENT." -- PAUL THE APOSTLE

WEEK ONE

WRITE IN A GENERAL OVERVIEW OF YOUR WEEKLY MEMORY WORK TO GIVE
YOURSELF A WEEKLY AT-A-GLANCE OF YOUR WEEK AHEAD.

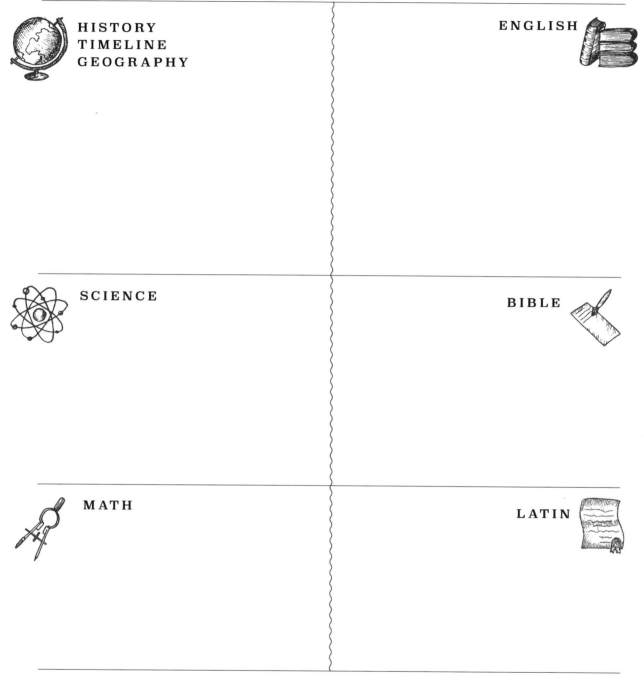

HISTORY
TIMELINE
GEOGRAPHY

ENGLISH

SCIENCE

BIBLE

MATH

LATIN

OTHER

HISTORY

Write your history memory work here 1-3 times.
Below, draw or paste a picture of this event.

GEOGRAPHY

W E E K L Y   T I M E L I N E

Label the year(s) and write the event in order from earliest (top) to latest (bottom). Draw a picture or paste a picture if you prefer to to it that way.

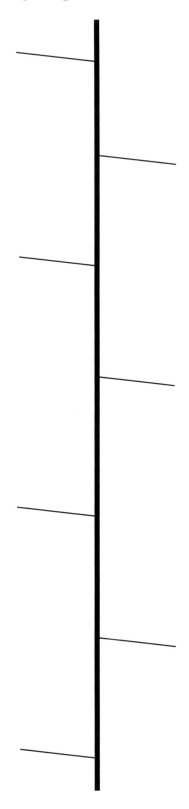

MATH

Copy your math memory work here:

Make your own math problems and solve them:

Make your own number math maze, game, or
simply copy the memory work again:

B I B L E

Copy your selected weekly Bible verse(s), hymn,
etc. below. Answer the questions below.

_____

_____

_____

_____

_____

_____

_____

What did you learn about in this passage?

Write a prayer with some of these words in it.

SCIENCE

Write your science memory work in the lines below. Answer the questions below and/or draw your own picture and label it using the memory work.

_____

_____

_____

_____

_____

_____

What do you know already? What do you want to know? What did you learn?

LATIN

Copy your Latin memory work and try to write
last week's information from memory.

THIS WEEK

LAST WEEK

ENGLISH

Write in your weekly memory work for English. Also, copy any advanced English memory work if it applies to you. Below, write some sentences that represent the memory work for the week.

Memory Work:

Write a sentence or short story that includes some of the memory work as an example. Or, diagram a sentence or two.

JOURNAL

HERITAGE

Week 2

"THE LORD IS GREATER THAN ALL: I HAVE SAID ENOUGH."

- SAINT PATRICK

WEEK TWO

HISTORY TIMELINE GEOGRAPHY

ENGLISH

SCIENCE

BIBLE

MATH

LATIN

OTHER

HISTORY

Write your history memory work here 1-3 times.
Below, draw or paste a picture of this event.

_____

_____

_____

_____

_____

_____

_____

GEOGRAPHY

21

WEEKLY TIMELINE

Label the year(s) and write the event in order from earliest (top) to latest (bottom). Draw a picture or paste a picture if you prefer to to it that way.

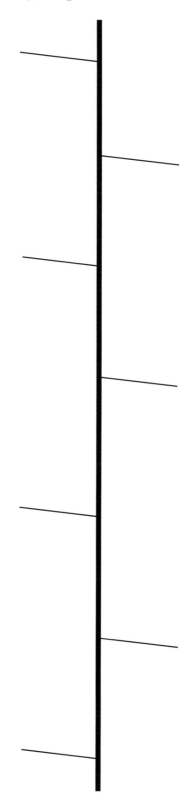

M A T H

Copy your math memory work here:

Make your own math problems and solve them:

~~~~~~

Make your own number math maze, game, or
simply copy the memory work again:

B I B L E

Copy your selected weekly Bible verse(s), hymn, etc. below. Answer the questions below.

_____

_____

_____

_____

_____

_____

_____

What did you learn about in this passage?

Write a prayer with some of these words in it.

SCIENCE

Write your science memory work in the lines below. Answer the questions below and/or draw your own picture and label it using the memory work.

_____

_____

_____

_____

_____

_____

What do you know already? What do you want to know? What did you learn?

L A T I N

Copy your Latin memory work and try to write
last week's information from memory.

T H I S   W E E K

L A S T   W E E K

E N G L I S H

Write in your weekly memory work for English.
Also, copy any advanced English memory work
if it applies to you. Below, write some sentences
that represent the memory work for the week.

Memory Work:

~~~~~~

Write a sentence or short story that includes
some of the memory work as an example.
Or, diagram a sentence or two.

JOURNAL

HERİTAGE

Week 3

"GOOD, BETTER, BEST. NEVER LET IT REST. 'TIL YOUR GOOD IS BETTER AND YOUR BETTER IS BEST." - SAINT JEROME

WEEK THREE

WRITE IN A GENERAL OVERVIEW OF YOUR WEEKLY MEMORY WORK TO GIVE
YOURSELF A WEEKLY AT-A-GLANCE OF YOUR WEEK AHEAD.

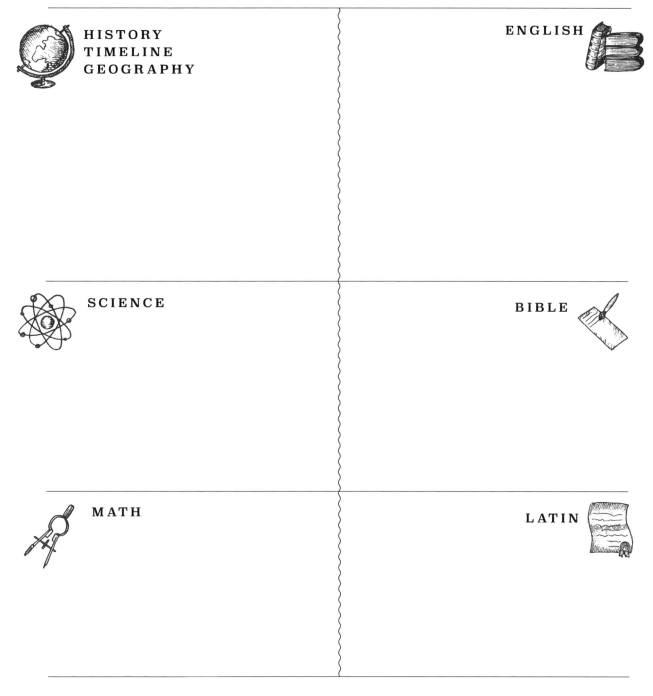

HISTORY
TIMELINE
GEOGRAPHY

ENGLISH

SCIENCE

BIBLE

MATH

LATIN

OTHER

HISTORY

Write your history memory work here 1-3 times.
Below, draw or paste a picture of this event.

_____

_____

_____

_____

_____

_____

_____

GEOGRAPHY

WEEKLY TIMELINE

Label the year(s) and write the event in order from earliest (top) to latest (bottom). Draw a picture or paste a picture if you prefer to to it that way.

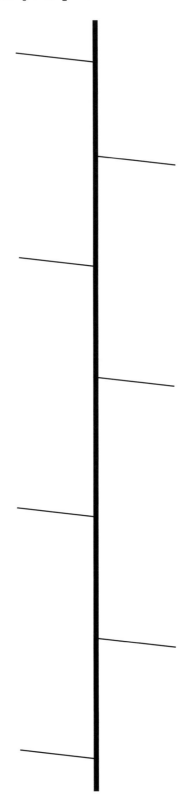

MATH

Copy your math memory work here:

Make your own math problems and solve them:

Make your own number math maze, game, or
simply copy the memory work again:

BIBLE

Copy your selected weekly Bible verse(s), hymn, etc. below. Answer the questions below.

_____

_____

_____

_____

_____

_____

_____

What did you learn about in this passage?

Write a prayer with some of these words in it.

SCIENCE

Write your science memory work in the lines below. Answer the questions below and/or draw your own picture and label it using the memory work.

_____

_____

_____

_____

_____

_____

What do you know already? What do you want to know? What did you learn?

LATIN

Copy your Latin memory work and try to write
last week's information from memory.

THIS WEEK

LAST WEEK

ENGLISH

Write in your weekly memory work for English.
Also, copy any advanced English memory work
if it applies to you. Below, write some sentences
that represent the memory work for the week.

Memory Work:

Write a sentence or short story that includes
some of the memory work as an example.
Or, diagram a sentence or two.

JOURNAL

HERITAGE

Week 4

"UNFURL THE SAILS, AND LET GOD STEER US WHERE HE WILL."
- VENERABLE BEDE

WEEK FOUR

WRITE IN A GENERAL OVERVIEW OF YOUR WEEKLY MEMORY WORK TO GIVE
YOURSELF A WEEKLY AT-A-GLANCE OF YOUR WEEK AHEAD.

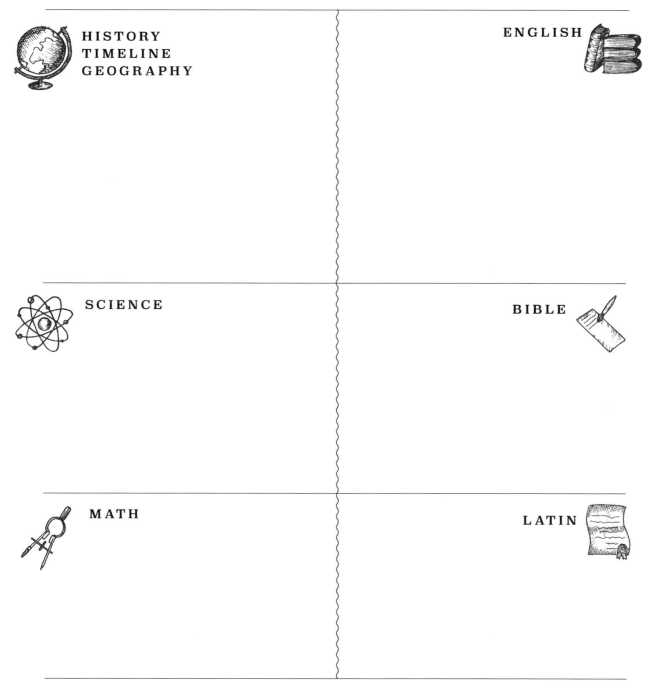

HISTORY
TIMELINE
GEOGRAPHY

ENGLISH

SCIENCE

BIBLE

MATH

LATIN

OTHER

HISTORY

Write your history memory work here 1-3 times.
Below, draw or paste a picture of this event.

GEOGRAPHY

WEEKLY TIMELINE

Label the year(s) and write the event in order from earliest (top) to latest (bottom). Draw a picture or paste a picture if you prefer to to it that way.

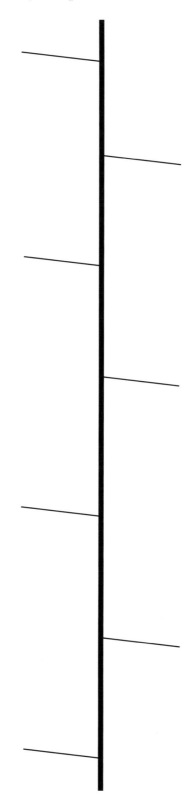

M A T H

Copy your math memory work here:

Make your own math problems and solve them:

~~~~~~

Make your own number math maze, game, or
simply copy the memory work again:

B I B L E

Copy your selected weekly Bible verse(s), hymn,
etc. below. Answer the questions below.

_____

_____

_____

_____

_____

_____

_____

What did you learn about in this passage?

Write a prayer with some of these words in it.

SCIENCE

Write your science memory work in the lines below. Answer the questions below and/or draw your own picture and label it using the memory work.

_____

_____

_____

_____

_____

_____

What do you know already? What do you want to know? What did you learn?

L A T I N

Copy your Latin memory work and try to write
last week's information from memory.

T H I S   W E E K

L A S T   W E E K

ENGLISH

Write in your weekly memory work for English.
Also, copy any advanced English memory work
if it applies to you. Below, write some sentences
that represent the memory work for the week.

Memory Work:

Write a sentence or short story that includes
some of the memory work as an example.
Or, diagram a sentence or two.

J O U R N A L

HERITAGE

Week 5

THE THINGS THAT WE LOVE TELL US WHAT WE ARE.
- THOMAS AQUINAS

WEEK FIVE

WRITE IN A GENERAL OVERVIEW OF YOUR WEEKLY MEMORY WORK TO GIVE
YOURSELF A WEEKLY AT-A-GLANCE OF YOUR WEEK AHEAD.

**HISTORY
TIMELINE
GEOGRAPHY**

ENGLISH

SCIENCE

BIBLE

MATH

LATIN

OTHER

HISTORY

Write your history memory work here 1-3 times.
Below, draw or paste a picture of this event.

_____

_____

_____

_____

_____

_____

_____

GEOGRAPHY

WEEKLY TIMELINE

Label the year(s) and write the event in order from
earliest (top) to latest (bottom). Draw a picture or paste a
picture if you prefer to to it that way.

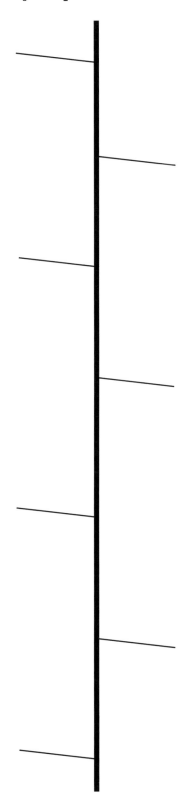

M A T H

Copy your math memory work here:

Make your own math problems and solve them:

~~~~~~

Make your own number math maze, game, or simply copy the memory work again:

BIBLE

Copy your selected weekly Bible verse(s), hymn,
etc. below. Answer the questions below.

_____

_____

_____

_____

_____

_____

_____

What did you learn about in this passage?

Write a prayer with some of these words in it.

SCIENCE

Write your science memory work in the lines
below. Answer the questions below and/or draw your
own picture and label it using the memory work.

_____

_____

_____

_____

_____

_____

What do you know already? What do you want to
know? What did you learn?

L A T I N

Copy your Latin memory work and try to write
last week's information from memory.

T H I S   W E E K

L A S T   W E E K

ENGLISH

Write in your weekly memory work for English.
Also, copy any advanced English memory work
if it applies to you. Below, write some sentences
that represent the memory work for the week.

Memory Work:

Write a sentence or short story that includes
some of the memory work as an example.
Or, diagram a sentence or two.

JOURNAL

WEEK SIX

WRITE IN A GENERAL OVERVIEW OF YOUR WEEKLY MEMORY WORK TO GIVE
YOURSELF A WEEKLY AT-A-GLANCE OF YOUR WEEK AHEAD.

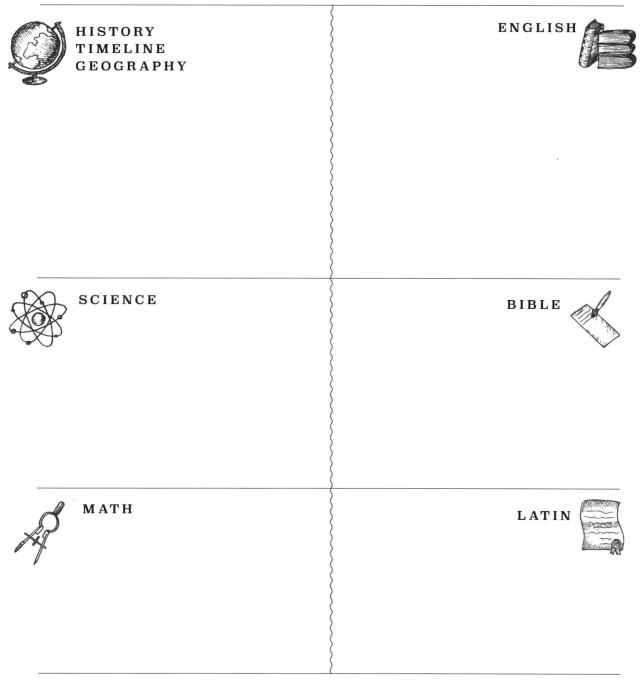

HISTORY
TIMELINE
GEOGRAPHY

ENGLISH

SCIENCE

BIBLE

MATH

LATIN

OTHER

H I S T O R Y

Write your history memory work here 1-3 times.
Below, draw or paste a picture of this event.

_____

_____

_____

_____

_____

_____

_____

_____

GEOGRAPHY

W E E K L Y   T I M E L I N E

Label the year(s) and write the event in order from earliest (top) to latest (bottom). Draw a picture or paste a picture if you prefer to to it that way.

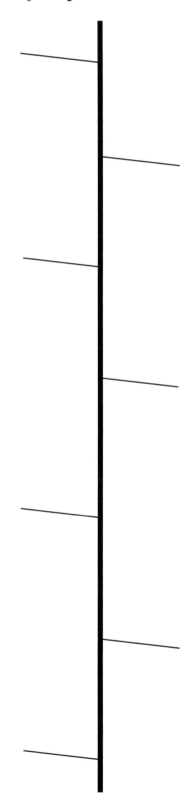

M A T H

Copy your math memory work here:

Make your own math problems and solve them:

~~~~~~

Make your own number math maze, game, or
simply copy the memory work again:

BIBLE

Copy your selected weekly Bible verse(s), hymn,
etc. below. Answer the questions below.

_____

_____

_____

_____

_____

_____

_____

What did you learn about in this passage?

Write a prayer with some of these words in it.

SCIENCE

Write your science memory work in the lines below. Answer the questions below and/or draw your own picture and label it using the memory work.

_____

_____

_____

_____

_____

_____

What do you know already? What do you want to know? What did you learn?

L A T I N

Copy your Latin memory work and try to write
last week's information from memory.

T H I S   W E E K

L A S T   W E E K

ENGLISH

Write in your weekly memory work for English.
Also, copy any advanced English memory work
if it applies to you. Below, write some sentences
that represent the memory work for the week.

Memory Work:

Write a sentence or short story that includes
some of the memory work as an example.
Or, diagram a sentence or two.

JOURNAL

Week 7

"EVERYTHING THAT IS DONE IN THE WORLD IS DONE BY HOPE.
-MARTIN LUTHER

WEEK SEVEN

WRITE IN A GENERAL OVERVIEW OF YOUR WEEKLY MEMORY WORK TO GIVE
YOURSELF A WEEKLY AT-A-GLANCE OF YOUR WEEK AHEAD.

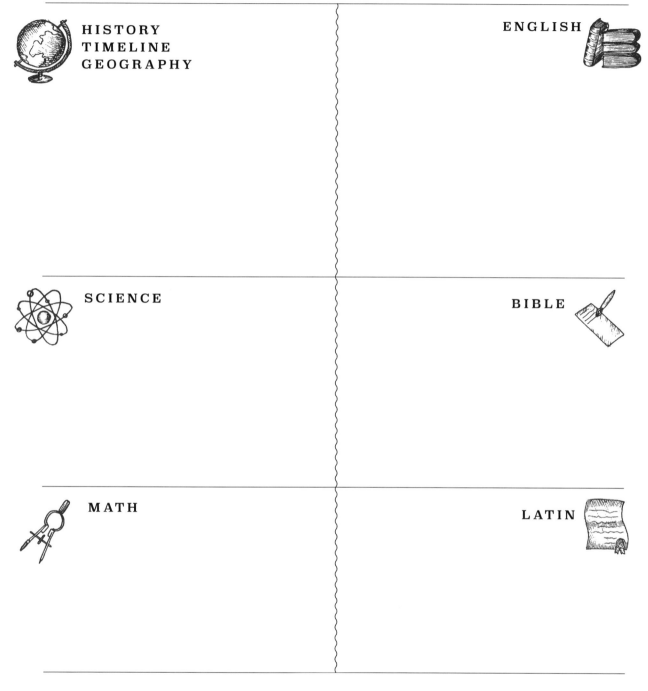

HISTORY
TIMELINE
GEOGRAPHY

ENGLISH

SCIENCE

BIBLE

MATH

LATIN

OTHER

HISTORY

Write your history memory work here 1-3 times.
Below, draw or paste a picture of this event.

GEOGRAPHY

WEEKLY TIMELINE

Label the year(s) and write the event in order from earliest (top) to latest (bottom). Draw a picture or paste a picture if you prefer to to it that way.

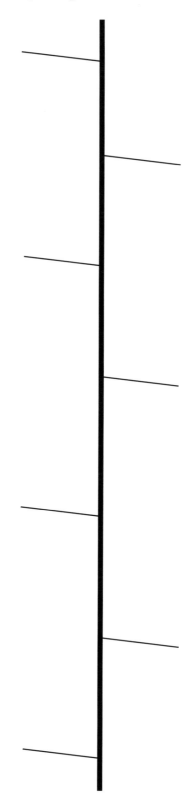

M A T H

Copy your math memory work here:

Make your own math problems and solve them:

〜〜〜〜〜〜〜〜〜〜〜〜〜〜〜〜〜〜〜〜〜〜〜〜〜〜〜〜〜〜〜〜

Make your own number math maze, game, or
simply copy the memory work again:

B I B L E

Copy your selected weekly Bible verse(s), hymn,
etc. below. Answer the questions below.

_____

_____

_____

_____

_____

_____

_____

What did you learn about in this passage?

Write a prayer with some of these words in it.

SCIENCE

Write your science memory work in the lines below. Answer the questions below and/or draw your own picture and label it using the memory work.

_____

_____

_____

_____

_____

_____

What do you know already? What do you want to know? What did you learn?

L A T I N

Copy your Latin memory work and try to write
last week's information from memory.

T H I S   W E E K

L A S T   W E E K

ENGLISH

Write in your weekly memory work for English.
Also, copy any advanced English memory work
if it applies to you. Below, write some sentences
that represent the memory work for the week.

Memory Work:

Write a sentence or short story that includes
some of the memory work as an example.
Or, diagram a sentence or two.

J O U R N A L

HERÍTAGE

Week 8

"THERE IS NO WORK BETTER THAN TO PLEASE GOD; TO POUR WATER, TO WASH DISHES, TO BE A COBBLER, OR AN APOSTLE, ALL ARE ONE; TO WASH DISHES AND TO PREACH ARE ALL ONE, AS TOUCHING THE DEED, TO PLEASE GOD." - WILLIAM TYNDALE

WEEK EIGHT

WRITE IN A GENERAL OVERVIEW OF YOUR WEEKLY MEMORY WORK TO GIVE
YOURSELF A WEEKLY AT-A-GLANCE OF YOUR WEEK AHEAD.

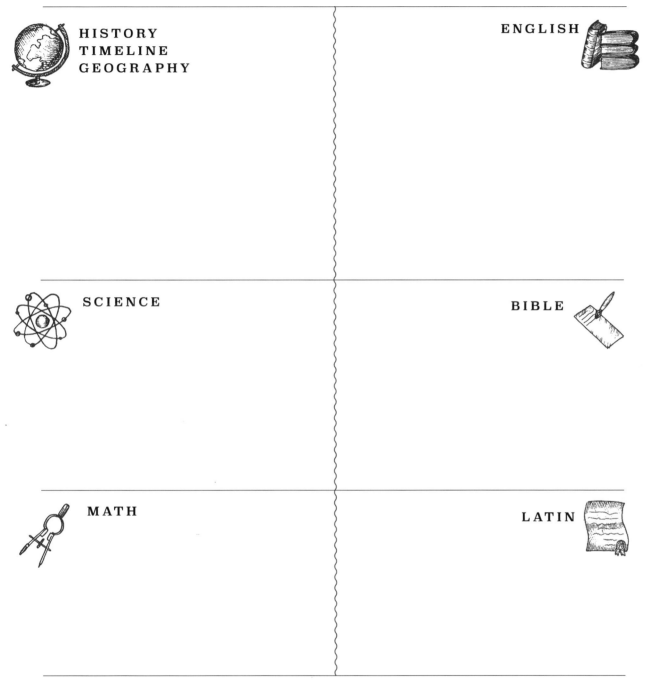

HISTORY
TIMELINE
GEOGRAPHY

ENGLISH

SCIENCE

BIBLE

MATH

LATIN

OTHER

HISTORY

Write your history memory work here 1-3 times.
Below, draw or paste a picture of this event.

GEOGRAPHY

WEEKLY TIMELINE

Label the year(s) and write the event in order from earliest (top) to latest (bottom). Draw a picture or paste a picture if you prefer to to it that way.

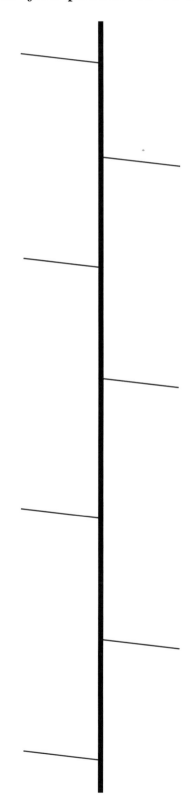

M A T H

Copy your math memory work here:

Make your own math problems and solve them:

~~~~~~

Make your own number math maze, game, or
simply copy the memory work again:

BIBLE

Copy your selected weekly Bible verse(s), hymn,
etc. below. Answer the questions below.

_____

_____

_____

_____

_____

_____

_____

What did you learn about in this passage?

Write a prayer with some of these words in it.

SCIENCE

Write your science memory work in the lines below. Answer the questions below and/or draw your own picture and label it using the memory work.

_____

_____

_____

_____

_____

_____

What do you know already? What do you want to know? What did you learn?

WEEK 8

L A T I N

_____

Copy your Latin memory work and try to write
last week's information from memory.

T H I S   W E E K

L A S T   W E E K

86

ENGLISH

Write in your weekly memory work for English.
Also, copy any advanced English memory work
if it applies to you. Below, write some sentences
that represent the memory work for the week.

Memory Work:

Write a sentence or short story that includes
some of the memory work as an example.
Or, diagram a sentence or two.

JOURNAL

HERITAGE

Week 9

"HUMILITY IS THE BEGINNING OF TRUE INTELLIGENCE." -JOHN CALVIN

WEEK NINE

WRITE IN A GENERAL OVERVIEW OF YOUR WEEKLY MEMORY WORK TO GIVE
YOURSELF A WEEKLY AT-A-GLANCE OF YOUR WEEK AHEAD.

**HISTORY
TIMELINE
GEOGRAPHY**

ENGLISH

SCIENCE

BIBLE

MATH

LATIN

OTHER

HISTORY

Write your history memory work here 1-3 times.
Below, draw or paste a picture of this event.

_____

_____

_____

_____

_____

_____

_____

_____

GEOGRAPHY

WEEKLY TIMELINE

Label the year(s) and write the event in order from earliest (top) to latest (bottom). Draw a picture or paste a picture if you prefer to to it that way.

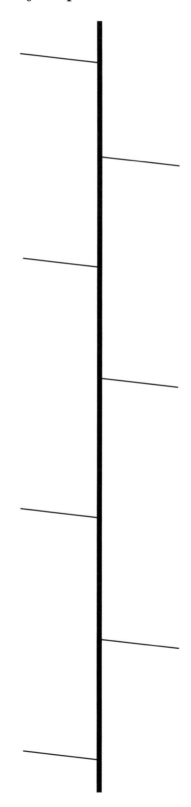

MATH

Copy your math memory work here:

Make your own math problems and solve them:

Make your own number math maze, game, or
simply copy the memory work again:

BIBLE

Copy your selected weekly Bible verse(s), hymn, etc. below. Answer the questions below.

_____

_____

_____

_____

_____

_____

_____

What did you learn about in this passage?

Write a prayer with some of these words in it.

SCIENCE

Write your science memory work in the lines below. Answer the questions below and/or draw your own picture and label it using the memory work.

_____

_____

_____

_____

_____

_____

What do you know already? What do you want to know? What did you learn?

L A T I N

Copy your Latin memory work and try to write
last week's information from memory.

T H I S   W E E K

L A S T   W E E K

ENGLISH

Write in your weekly memory work for English.
Also, copy any advanced English memory work
if it applies to you. Below, write some sentences
that represent the memory work for the week.

Memory Work:

Write a sentence or short story that includes
some of the memory work as an example.
Or, diagram a sentence or two.

J O U R N A L

HERITAGE

Week 10

"OH, HOW PRECIOUS IS TIME, AND HOW IT PAINS ME TO SEE IT SLIDE AWAY, WHILE I DO SO LITTLE TO ANY GOOD PURPOSE." - DAVID BRAINERD

WEEK TEN

WRITE IN A GENERAL OVERVIEW OF YOUR WEEKLY MEMORY WORK TO GIVE
YOURSELF A WEEKLY AT-A-GLANCE OF YOUR WEEK AHEAD.

**HISTORY
TIMELINE
GEOGRAPHY**

ENGLISH

SCIENCE

BIBLE

MATH

LATIN

OTHER

HISTORY

Write your history memory work here 1-3 times.
Below, draw or paste a picture of this event.

_____

_____

_____

_____

_____

_____

_____

_____

GEOGRAPHY

WEEKLY TIMELINE

Label the year(s) and write the event in order from
earliest (top) to latest (bottom). Draw a picture or paste a
picture if you prefer to to it that way.

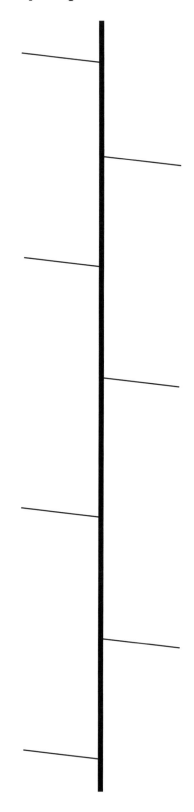

MATH

Copy your math memory work here:

Make your own math problems and solve them:

~~~~~~

Make your own number math maze, game, or
simply copy the memory work again:

BIBLE

Copy your selected weekly Bible verse(s), hymn, etc. below. Answer the questions below.

_____

_____

_____

_____

_____

_____

_____

What did you learn about in this passage?

Write a prayer with some of these words in it.

SCIENCE

Write your science memory work in the lines below. Answer the questions below and/or draw your own picture and label it using the memory work.

_____

_____

_____

_____

_____

_____

What do you know already? What do you want to know? What did you learn?

L A T I N

Copy your Latin memory work and try to write
last week's information from memory.

T H I S   W E E K

L A S T   W E E K

E N G L I S H

Write in your weekly memory work for English.
Also, copy any advanced English memory work
if it applies to you. Below, write some sentences
that represent the memory work for the week.

Memory Work:

Write a sentence or short story that includes
some of the memory work as an example.
Or, diagram a sentence or two.

JOURNAL

HERITAGE

Week 11

"EXPECT GREAT THINGS FROM GOD, ATTEMPT GREAT THINGS FOR GOD."
- WILLIAM CAREY

WEEK ELEVEN

WRITE IN A GENERAL OVERVIEW OF YOUR WEEKLY MEMORY WORK TO GIVE
YOURSELF A WEEKLY AT-A-GLANCE OF YOUR WEEK AHEAD.

**HISTORY
TIMELINE
GEOGRAPHY**

ENGLISH

SCIENCE

BIBLE

MATH

LATIN

OTHER

HISTORY

Write your history memory work here 1-3 times.
Below, draw or paste a picture of this event.

_____

_____

_____

_____

_____

_____

_____

_____

GEOGRAPHY

W E E K L Y   T I M E L I N E

Label the year(s) and write the event in order from earliest (top) to latest (bottom). Draw a picture or paste a picture if you prefer to to it that way.

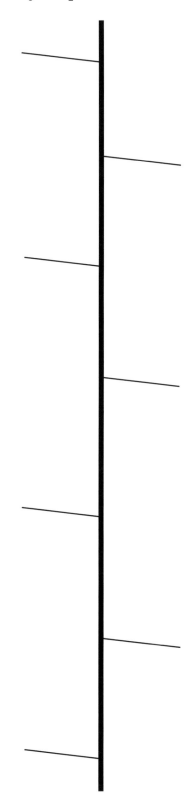

M A T H

Copy your math memory work here:

Make your own math problems and solve them:

Make your own number math maze, game, or
simply copy the memory work again:

BIBLE

Copy your selected weekly Bible verse(s), hymn, etc. below. Answer the questions below.

_____

_____

_____

_____

_____

_____

_____

What did you learn about in this passage?

Write a prayer with some of these words in it.

SCIENCE

Write your science memory work in the lines below. Answer the questions below and/or draw your own picture and label it using the memory work.

_____

_____

_____

_____

_____

_____

What do you know already? What do you want to know? What did you learn?

L A T I N

Copy your Latin memory work and try to write
last week's information from memory.

T H I S   W E E K

L A S T   W E E K

ENGLISH

Write in your weekly memory work for English.
Also, copy any advanced English memory work
if it applies to you. Below, write some sentences
that represent the memory work for the week.

Memory Work:

Write a sentence or short story that includes
some of the memory work as an example.
Or, diagram a sentence or two.

JOURNAL

Week 12

"DO ALL THE GOOD YOU CAN, BY ALL THE MEANS YOU CAN, IN ALL THE WAYS YOU CAN, IN ALL THE PLACES YOU CAN, AT ALL THE TIMES YOU CAN, TO ALL THE PEOPLE YOU CAN, AS LONG AS EVER YOU CAN." - JOHN WESLEY

WEEK TWELVE

WRITE IN A GENERAL OVERVIEW OF YOUR WEEKLY MEMORY WORK TO GIVE
YOURSELF A WEEKLY AT-A-GLANCE OF YOUR WEEK AHEAD.

HISTORY
TIMELINE
GEOGRAPHY

ENGLISH

SCIENCE

BIBLE

MATH

LATIN

OTHER

HISTORY

Write your history memory work here 1-3 times.
Below, draw or paste a picture of this event.

_____

_____

_____

_____

_____

_____

_____

G E O G R A P H Y

WEEKLY TIMELINE

Label the year(s) and write the event in order from earliest (top) to latest (bottom). Draw a picture or paste a picture if you prefer to to it that way.

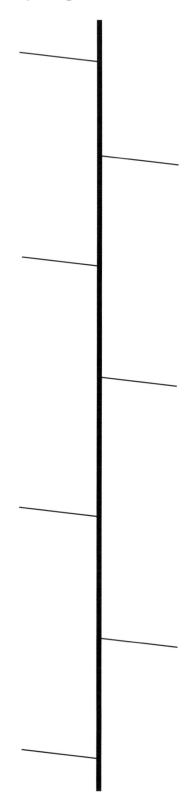

MATH

Copy your math memory work here:

Make your own math problems and solve them:

~~~~~~

Make your own number math maze, game, or
simply copy the memory work again:

BIBLE

Copy your selected weekly Bible verse(s), hymn, etc. below. Answer the questions below.

_____

_____

_____

_____

_____

_____

_____

What did you learn about in this passage?

Write a prayer with some of these words in it.

SCIENCE

Write your science memory work in the lines
below. Answer the questions below and/or draw your
own picture and label it using the memory work.

_____

_____

_____

_____

_____

_____

What do you know already? What do you want to
know? What did you learn?

L A T I N

Copy your Latin memory work and try to write
last week's information from memory.

T H I S   W E E K

L A S T   W E E K

ENGLISH

Write in your weekly memory work for English.
Also, copy any advanced English memory work
if it applies to you. Below, write some sentences
that represent the memory work for the week.

Memory Work:

Write a sentence or short story that includes
some of the memory work as an example.
Or, diagram a sentence or two.

JOURNAL

HERITAGE

Week 13

"IF WE ARE INTERESTED IN CHRIST BY FAITH, NOTWITHSTANDING OUR IMPERFECTIONS AND SINS, GOD WILL BE OUR GOD THROUGH GRACE."
- ADONIRAM JUDSON

WEEK THIRTEEN

WRITE IN A GENERAL OVERVIEW OF YOUR WEEKLY MEMORY WORK TO GIVE
YOURSELF A WEEKLY AT-A-GLANCE OF YOUR WEEK AHEAD.

HISTORY
TIMELINE
GEOGRAPHY

ENGLISH

SCIENCE

BIBLE

MATH

LATIN

OTHER

HISTORY

Write your history memory work here 1-3 times.
Below, draw or paste a picture of this event.

GEOGRAPHY

WEEKLY TIMELINE

Label the year(s) and write the event in order from earliest (top) to latest (bottom). Draw a picture or paste a picture if you prefer to to it that way.

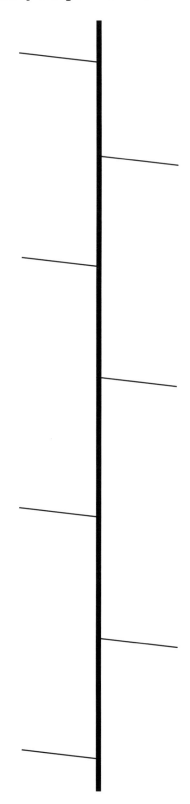

M A T H

Copy your math memory work here:

Make your own math problems and solve them:

~~~~~~

Make your own number math maze, game, or
simply copy the memory work again:

B I B L E

Copy your selected weekly Bible verse(s), hymn,
etc. below. Answer the questions below.

_____

_____

_____

_____

_____

_____

_____

What did you learn about in this passage?

Write a prayer with some of these words in it.

SCIENCE

Write your science memory work in the lines below. Answer the questions below and/or draw your own picture and label it using the memory work.

_____

_____

_____

_____

_____

_____

What do you know already? What do you want to know? What did you learn?

L A T I N

Copy your Latin memory work and try to write
last week's information from memory.

T H I S   W E E K

L A S T   W E E K

ENGLISH

Write in your weekly memory work for English.
Also, copy any advanced English memory work
if it applies to you. Below, write some sentences
that represent the memory work for the week.

Memory Work:

Write a sentence or short story that includes
some of the memory work as an example.
Or, diagram a sentence or two.

JOURNAL

HERITAGE

Week 14

"FEAR GOD AND WORK HARD." - DAVID LIVINGSTONE

WEEK FOURTEEN

WRITE IN A GENERAL OVERVIEW OF YOUR WEEKLY MEMORY WORK TO GIVE
YOURSELF A WEEKLY AT-A-GLANCE OF YOUR WEEK AHEAD.

HISTORY
TIMELINE
GEOGRAPHY

ENGLISH

SCIENCE

BIBLE

MATH

LATIN

OTHER

HISTORY

Write your history memory work here 1-3 times.
Below, draw or paste a picture of this event.

GEOGRAPHY

WEEKLY TIMELINE

Label the year(s) and write the event in order from earliest (top) to latest (bottom). Draw a picture or paste a picture if you prefer to to it that way.

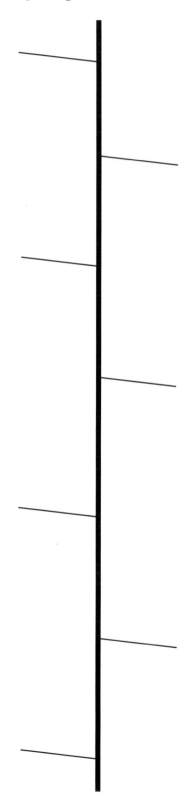

MATH

Copy your math memory work here:

Make your own math problems and solve them:

Make your own number math maze, game, or
simply copy the memory work again:

BIBLE

Copy your selected weekly Bible verse(s), hymn,
etc. below. Answer the questions below.

_____

_____

_____

_____

_____

_____

_____

What did you learn about in this passage?

Write a prayer with some of these words in it.

SCIENCE

Write your science memory work in the lines below. Answer the questions below and/or draw your own picture and label it using the memory work.

_____

_____

_____

_____

_____

_____

What do you know already? What do you want to know? What did you learn?

L A T I N

Copy your Latin memory work and try to write
last week's information from memory.

T H I S   W E E K

L A S T   W E E K

ENGLISH

Write in your weekly memory work for English.
Also, copy any advanced English memory work
if it applies to you. Below, write some sentences
that represent the memory work for the week.

Memory Work:

Write a sentence or short story that includes
some of the memory work as an example.
Or, diagram a sentence or two.

JOURNAL

Week 15

"IF WE ARE FAITHFUL TO GOD IN LITTLE THINGS, WE SHALL GAIN EXPERIENCE AND STRENGTH THAT WILL BE HELPFUL TO US IN THE MORE SERIOUS TRIALS OF LIFE." - HUDSON TAYLOR

WEEK FIFTEEN

WRITE IN A GENERAL OVERVIEW OF YOUR WEEKLY MEMORY WORK TO GIVE
YOURSELF A WEEKLY AT-A-GLANCE OF YOUR WEEK AHEAD.

HISTORY
TIMELINE
GEOGRAPHY

ENGLISH

SCIENCE

BIBLE

MATH

LATIN

OTHER

HISTORY

_____

Write your history memory work here 1-3 times.
Below, draw or paste a picture of this event.

_____

_____

_____

_____

_____

_____

_____

_____

GEOGRAPHY

W E E K L Y   T I M E L I N E

Label the year(s) and write the event in order from earliest (top) to latest (bottom). Draw a picture or paste a picture if you prefer to to it that way.

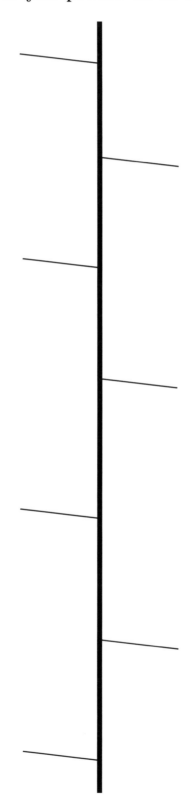

MATH

Copy your math memory work here:

Make your own math problems and solve them:

Make your own number math maze, game, or simply copy the memory work again:

BIBLE

Copy your selected weekly Bible verse(s), hymn, etc. below. Answer the questions below.

_____

_____

_____

_____

_____

_____

_____

What did you learn about in this passage?

Write a prayer with some of these words in it.

SCIENCE

Write your science memory work in the lines below. Answer the questions below and/or draw your own picture and label it using the memory work.

_____

_____

_____

_____

_____

What do you know already? What do you want to know? What did you learn?

L A T I N

Copy your Latin memory work and try to write
last week's information from memory.

T H I S   W E E K

L A S T   W E E K

ENGLISH

Write in your weekly memory work for English.
Also, copy any advanced English memory work
if it applies to you. Below, write some sentences
that represent the memory work for the week.

Memory Work:

Write a sentence or short story that includes
some of the memory work as an example.
Or, diagram a sentence or two.

JOURNAL

HERITAGE

Week 16

"PRAYER IS AS NATURAL AN EXPRESSION OF FAITH AS BREATHING IS OF LIFE." - JONATHAN EDWARDS

WEEK SIXTEEN

WRITE IN A GENERAL OVERVIEW OF YOUR WEEKLY MEMORY WORK TO GIVE
YOURSELF A WEEKLY AT-A-GLANCE OF YOUR WEEK AHEAD.

**HISTORY
TIMELINE
GEOGRAPHY**

ENGLISH

SCIENCE

BIBLE

MATH

LATIN

OTHER

HISTORY

Write your history memory work here 1-3 times.
Below, draw or paste a picture of this event.

_____

_____

_____

_____

_____

_____

_____

GEOGRAPHY

WEEKLY TIMELINE

Label the year(s) and write the event in order from earliest (top) to latest (bottom). Draw a picture or paste a picture if you prefer to to it that way.

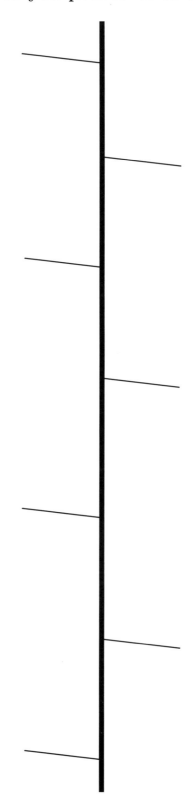

MATH

Copy your math memory work here:

Make your own math problems and solve them:

Make your own number math maze, game, or simply copy the memory work again:

BIBLE

Copy your selected weekly Bible verse(s), hymn,
etc. below. Answer the questions below.

_____

_____

_____

_____

_____

_____

_____

What did you learn about in this passage?

Write a prayer with some of these words in it.

SCIENCE

Write your science memory work in the lines below. Answer the questions below and/or draw your own picture and label it using the memory work.

_____

_____

_____

_____

_____

_____

What do you know already? What do you want to know? What did you learn?

L A T I N

Copy your Latin memory work and try to write
last week's information from memory.

T H I S   W E E K

L A S T   W E E K

ENGLISH

Write in your weekly memory work for English.
Also, copy any advanced English memory work
if it applies to you. Below, write some sentences
that represent the memory work for the week.

Memory Work:

Write a sentence or short story that includes
some of the memory work as an example.
Or, diagram a sentence or two.

JOURNAL

HERITAGE

Week 17

"THE LESS WE READ THE WORD OF GOD, THE LESS WE DESIRE TO READ IT, AND THE LESS WE PRAY, THE LESS WE DESIRE TO PRAY."
- GEORGE MULLER

WEEK SEVENTEEN

WRITE IN A GENERAL OVERVIEW OF YOUR WEEKLY MEMORY WORK TO GIVE
YOURSELF A WEEKLY AT-A-GLANCE OF YOUR WEEK AHEAD.

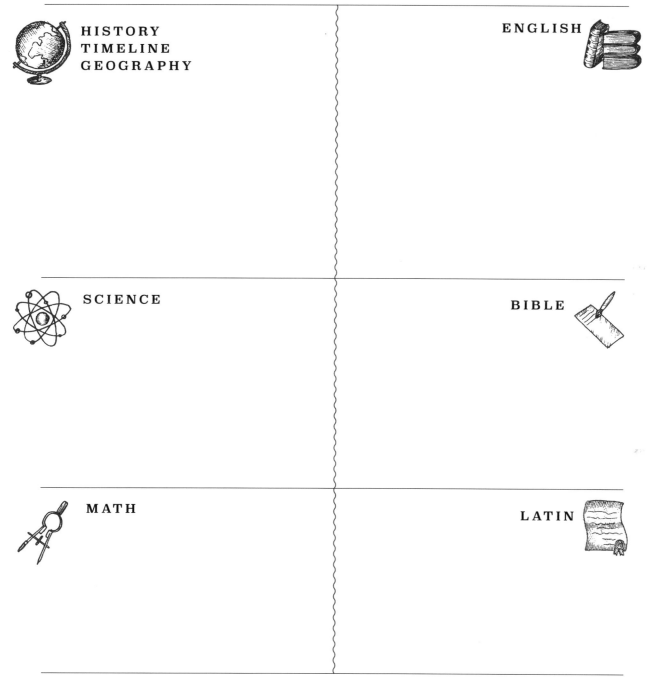

HISTORY
TIMELINE
GEOGRAPHY

ENGLISH

SCIENCE

BIBLE

MATH

LATIN

OTHER

HISTORY

Write your history memory work here 1-3 times.
Below, draw or paste a picture of this event.

GEOGRAPHY

WEEKLY TIMELINE

Label the year(s) and write the event in order from earliest (top) to latest (bottom). Draw a picture or paste a picture if you prefer to to it that way.

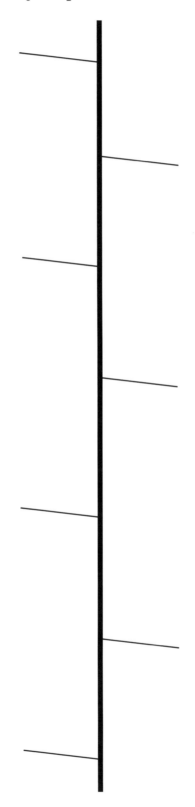

MATH

Copy your math memory work here:

Make your own math problems and solve them:

~~~~~~

Make your own number math maze, game, or simply copy the memory work again:

BIBLE

Copy your selected weekly Bible verse(s), hymn,
etc. below. Answer the questions below.

_____

_____

_____

_____

_____

_____

_____

What did you learn about in this passage?

Write a prayer with some of these words in it.

SCIENCE

Write your science memory work in the lines below. Answer the questions below and/or draw your own picture and label it using the memory work.

_____

_____

_____

_____

_____

_____

What do you know already? What do you want to know? What did you learn?

L A T I N

Copy your Latin memory work and try to write
last week's information from memory.

T H I S   W E E K

L A S T   W E E K

ENGLISH

Write in your weekly memory work for English.
Also, copy any advanced English memory work
if it applies to you. Below, write some sentences
that represent the memory work for the week.

Memory Work:

Write a sentence or short story that includes
some of the memory work as an example.
Or, diagram a sentence or two.

J O U R N A L

Week 18

"CHRIST NEVER WAS IN A HURRY. THERE WAS NO RUSHING FORWARD, NO ANTICIPATING, NO FRETTING OVER WHAT MIGHT BE. EACH DAY'S DUTIES WERE DONE AS EACH DAY BROUGHT THEM, AND THE REST WAS LEFT WITH GOD." - MARY SLESSOR

WEEK EIGHTEEN

WRITE IN A GENERAL OVERVIEW OF YOUR WEEKLY MEMORY WORK TO GIVE
YOURSELF A WEEKLY AT-A-GLANCE OF YOUR WEEK AHEAD.

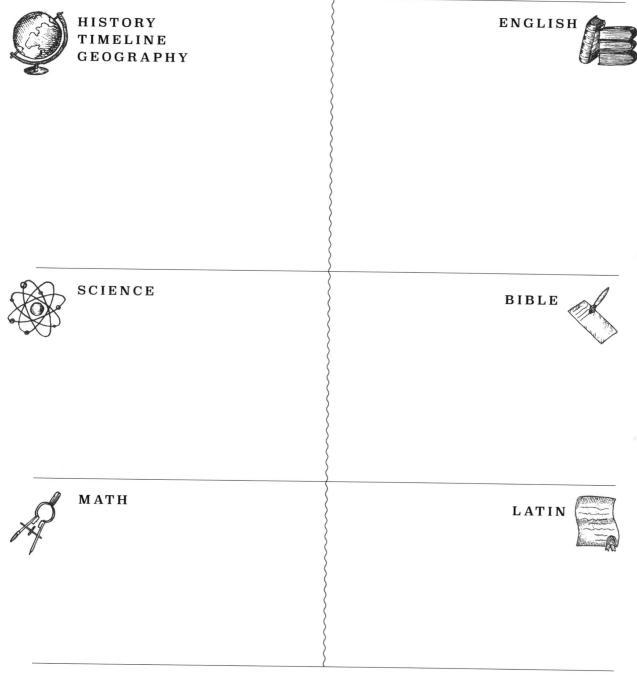

**HISTORY
TIMELINE
GEOGRAPHY**

ENGLISH

SCIENCE

BIBLE

MATH

LATIN

OTHER

HISTORY

Write your history memory work here 1-3 times.
Below, draw or paste a picture of this event.

GEOGRAPHY

WEEKLY TIMELINE

Label the year(s) and write the event in order from earliest (top) to latest (bottom). Draw a picture or paste a picture if you prefer to to it that way.

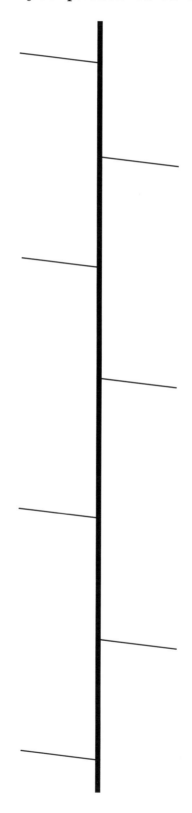

MATH

Copy your math memory work here:

Make your own math problems and solve them:

~~~~~~

Make your own number math maze, game, or simply copy the memory work again:

BIBLE

Copy your selected weekly Bible verse(s), hymn, etc. below. Answer the questions below.

_____

_____

_____

_____

_____

_____

_____

What did you learn about in this passage?

Write a prayer with some of these words in it.

SCIENCE

Write your science memory work in the lines
below. Answer the questions below and/or draw your
own picture and label it using the memory work.

_____

_____

_____

_____

_____

_____

What do you know already? What do you want to
know? What did you learn?

L A T I N

Copy your Latin memory work and try to write
last week's information from memory.

T H I S   W E E K

L A S T   W E E K

ENGLISH

Write in your weekly memory work for English.
Also, copy any advanced English memory work
if it applies to you. Below, write some sentences
that represent the memory work for the week.

Memory Work:

Write a sentence or short story that includes
some of the memory work as an example.
Or, diagram a sentence or two.

JOURNAL

Week 19

"LET NOTHING BE SAID ABOUT ANYONE UNLESS IT PASSES THROUGH THE THREE SIEVES: IS IT TRUE? IS IT KIND? IS IT NECESSARY?"
- AMY CARMICHAEL

WEEK NINETEEN

WRITE IN A GENERAL OVERVIEW OF YOUR WEEKLY MEMORY WORK TO GIVE
YOURSELF A WEEKLY AT-A-GLANCE OF YOUR WEEK AHEAD.

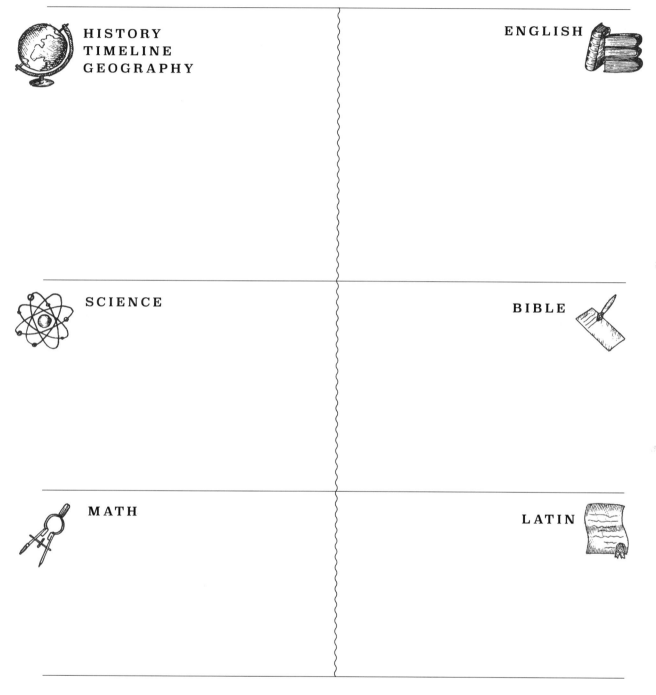

**HISTORY
TIMELINE
GEOGRAPHY**

ENGLISH

SCIENCE

BIBLE

MATH

LATIN

OTHER

HISTORY

Write your history memory work here 1-3 times.
Below, draw or paste a picture of this event.

GEOGRAPHY

WEEKLY TIMELINE

Label the year(s) and write the event in order from earliest (top) to latest (bottom). Draw a picture or paste a picture if you prefer to to it that way.

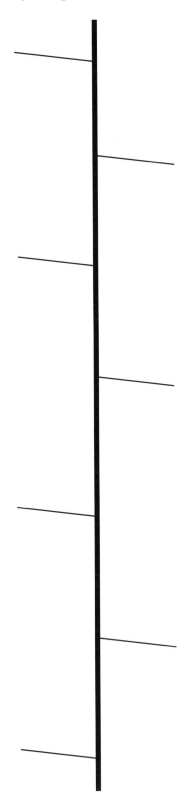

MATH

Copy your math memory work here:

Make your own math problems and solve them:

~~~~~~

Make your own number math maze, game, or simply copy the memory work again:

BIBLE

Copy your selected weekly Bible verse(s), hymn,
etc. below. Answer the questions below.

_____

_____

_____

_____

_____

_____

_____

What did you learn about in this passage?

Write a prayer with some of these words in it.

SCIENCE

Write your science memory work in the lines below. Answer the questions below and/or draw your own picture and label it using the memory work.

_____

_____

_____

_____

_____

_____

What do you know already? What do you want to know? What did you learn?

LATIN

Copy your Latin memory work and try to write
last week's information from memory.

THIS WEEK

LAST WEEK

ENGLISH

Write in your weekly memory work for English. Also, copy any advanced English memory work if it applies to you. Below, write some sentences that represent the memory work for the week.

Memory Work:

Write a sentence or short story that includes some of the memory work as an example. Or, diagram a sentence or two.

JOURNAL

HERİTAGE

Week 20

"LORD, GIVE ME FIRMNESS WITHOUT HARDNESS, STEADFASTNESS WITHOUT DOGMATISM, LOVE WITHOUT WEAKNESS."
- JIM ELLIOT

WEEK TWENTY

WRITE IN A GENERAL OVERVIEW OF YOUR WEEKLY MEMORY WORK TO GIVE
YOURSELF A WEEKLY AT-A-GLANCE OF YOUR WEEK AHEAD.

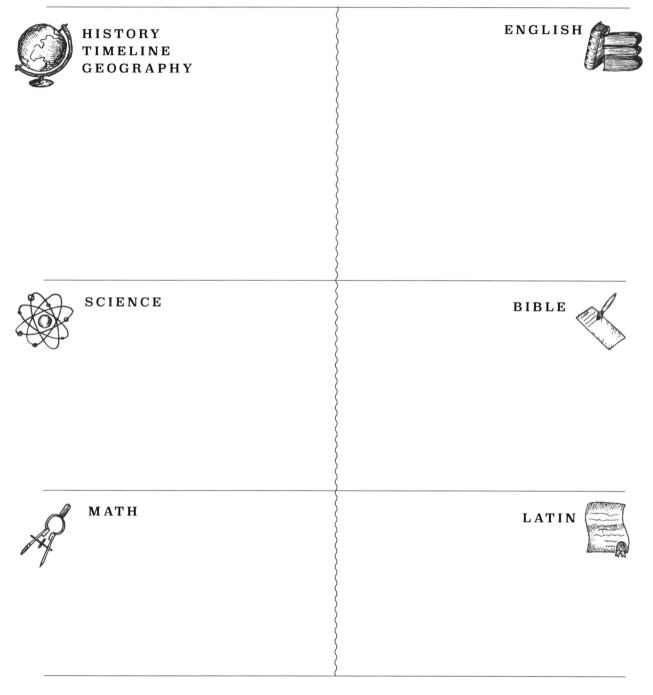

HISTORY
TIMELINE
GEOGRAPHY

ENGLISH

SCIENCE

BIBLE

MATH

LATIN

OTHER

HISTORY

Write your history memory work here 1-3 times.
Below, draw or paste a picture of this event.

G E O G R A P H Y

WEEKLY TIMELINE

Label the year(s) and write the event in order from earliest (top) to latest (bottom). Draw a picture or paste a picture if you prefer to to it that way.

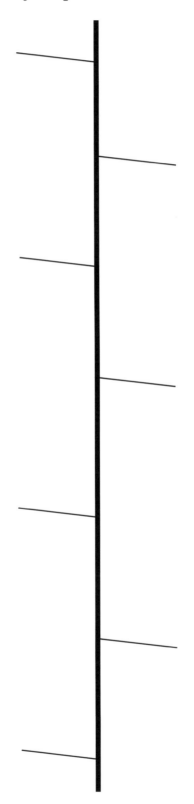

MATH

Copy your math memory work here:

Make your own math problems and solve them:

~~~~~~

Make your own number math maze, game, or simply copy the memory work again:

BIBLE

Copy your selected weekly Bible verse(s), hymn, etc. below. Answer the questions below.

_____

_____

_____

_____

_____

_____

_____

What did you learn about in this passage?

Write a prayer with some of these words in it.

SCIENCE

Write your science memory work in the lines below. Answer the questions below and/or draw your own picture and label it using the memory work.

_____

_____

_____

_____

_____

What do you know already? What do you want to know? What did you learn?

LATIN

Copy your Latin memory work and try to write
last week's information from memory.

THIS WEEK

LAST WEEK

ENGLISH

Write in your weekly memory work for English.
Also, copy any advanced English memory work
if it applies to you. Below, write some sentences
that represent the memory work for the week.

Memory Work:

Write a sentence or short story that includes
some of the memory work as an example.
Or, diagram a sentence or two.

JOURNAL

HERİTAGE

Week 21

"THE EAGLE THAT SOARS IN THE UPPER AIR DOES NOT WORRY ITSELF
HOW IT IS TO CROSS RIVERS." - GLADYS AYLWARD

WEEK TWENTY-ONE

WRITE IN A GENERAL OVERVIEW OF YOUR WEEKLY MEMORY WORK TO GIVE
YOURSELF A WEEKLY AT-A-GLANCE OF YOUR WEEK AHEAD.

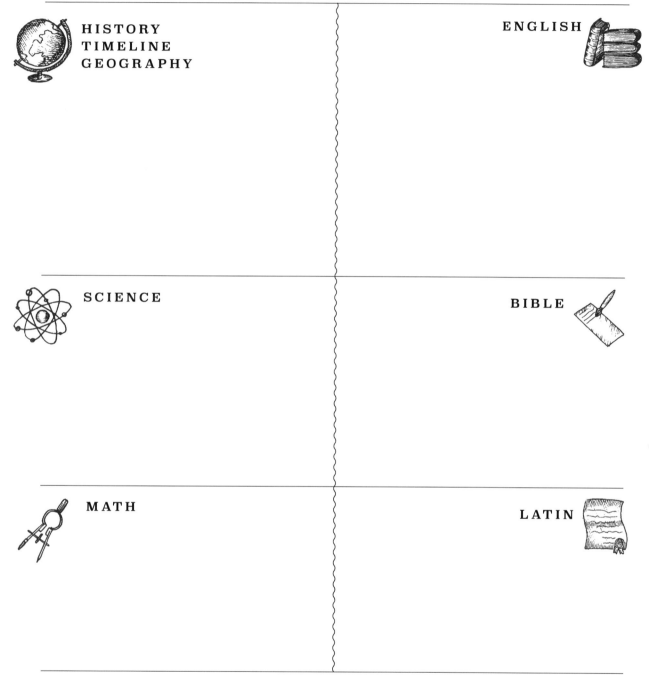

HISTORY
TIMELINE
GEOGRAPHY

ENGLISH

SCIENCE

BIBLE

MATH

LATIN

OTHER

HISTORY

Write your history memory work here 1-3 times.
Below, draw or paste a picture of this event.

_____

_____

_____

_____

_____

_____

_____

_____

GEOGRAPHY

WEEKLY TIMELINE

Label the year(s) and write the event in order from earliest (top) to latest (bottom). Draw a picture or paste a picture if you prefer to to it that way.

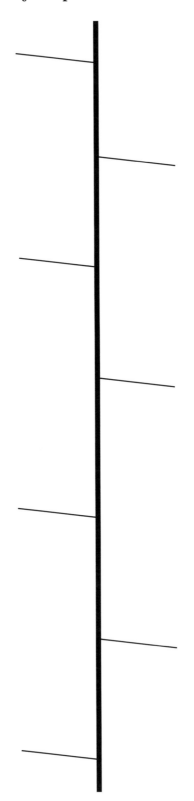

MATH

Copy your math memory work here:

Make your own math problems and solve them:

Make your own number math maze, game, or
simply copy the memory work again:

BIBLE

Copy your selected weekly Bible verse(s), hymn,
etc. below. Answer the questions below.

_____

_____

_____

_____

_____

_____

_____

What did you learn about in this passage?

Write a prayer with some of these words in it.

SCIENCE

Write your science memory work in the lines below. Answer the questions below and/or draw your own picture and label it using the memory work.

_____

_____

_____

_____

_____

_____

What do you know already? What do you want to know? What did you learn?

L A T I N

Copy your Latin memory work and try to write
last week's information from memory.

T H I S   W E E K

L A S T   W E E K

ENGLISH

Write in your weekly memory work for English.
Also, copy any advanced English memory work
if it applies to you. Below, write some sentences
that represent the memory work for the week.

Memory Work:

Write a sentence or short story that includes
some of the memory work as an example.
Or, diagram a sentence or two.

J O U R N A L

Week 22

"IF YOU ARE NOT GUIDED BY GOD, YOU WILL BE GUIDED BY SOMETHING OR SOMEONE ELSE." - ERIC LIDDELL

WEEK TWENTY-TWO

WRITE IN A GENERAL OVERVIEW OF YOUR WEEKLY MEMORY WORK TO GIVE
YOURSELF A WEEKLY AT-A-GLANCE OF YOUR WEEK AHEAD.

HISTORY
TIMELINE
GEOGRAPHY

ENGLISH

SCIENCE

BIBLE

MATH

LATIN

OTHER

HISTORY

Write your history memory work here 1-3 times.
Below, draw or paste a picture of this event.

G E O G R A P H Y

WEEKLY TIMELINE

Label the year(s) and write the event in order from
earliest (top) to latest (bottom). Draw a picture or paste a
picture if you prefer to to it that way.

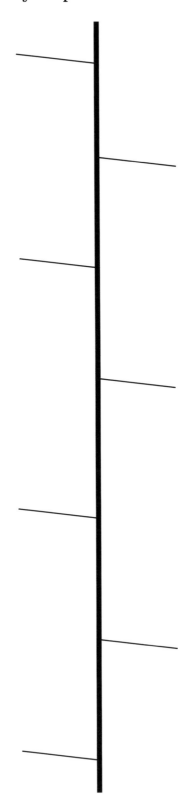

MATH

Copy your math memory work here:

Make your own math problems and solve them:

~~~~~~

Make your own number math maze, game, or
simply copy the memory work again:

BIBLE

Copy your selected weekly Bible verse(s), hymn,
etc. below. Answer the questions below.

_____

_____

_____

_____

_____

_____

_____

What did you learn about in this passage?

Write a prayer with some of these words in it.

SCIENCE

Write your science memory work in the lines below. Answer the questions below and/or draw your own picture and label it using the memory work.

_____

_____

_____

_____

_____

_____

What do you know already? What do you want to know? What did you learn?

L A T I N

Copy your Latin memory work and try to write
last week's information from memory.

T H I S   W E E K

L A S T   W E E K

ENGLISH

Write in your weekly memory work for English.
Also, copy any advanced English memory work
if it applies to you. Below, write some sentences
that represent the memory work for the week.

Memory Work:

~~~~~~

Write a sentence or short story that includes
some of the memory work as an example.
Or, diagram a sentence or two.

J O U R N A L

HERİTAGE

Week 23

"SEEK TO GIVE MUCH - EXPECT NOTHING." - JONATHAN GOFORTH

WEEK TWENTY-THREE

WRITE IN A GENERAL OVERVIEW OF YOUR WEEKLY MEMORY WORK TO GIVE
YOURSELF A WEEKLY AT-A-GLANCE OF YOUR WEEK AHEAD.

HISTORY
TIMELINE
GEOGRAPHY

ENGLISH

SCIENCE

BIBLE

MATH

LATIN

OTHER

HISTORY

Write your history memory work here 1-3 times.
Below, draw or paste a picture of this event.

_____

_____

_____

_____

_____

_____

_____

_____

GEOGRAPHY

WEEKLY TIMELINE

Label the year(s) and write the event in order from earliest (top) to latest (bottom). Draw a picture or paste a picture if you prefer to to it that way.

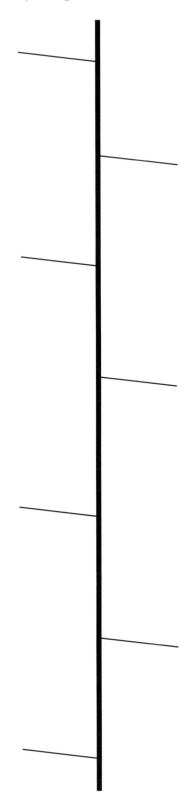

MATH

Copy your math memory work here:

Make your own math problems and solve them:

~~~~~~

Make your own number math maze, game, or simply copy the memory work again:

BIBLE

Copy your selected weekly Bible verse(s), hymn, etc. below. Answer the questions below.

_____

_____

_____

_____

_____

_____

_____

What did you learn about in this passage?

Write a prayer with some of these words in it.

SCIENCE

Write your science memory work in the lines below. Answer the questions below and/or draw your own picture and label it using the memory work.

_____

_____

_____

_____

_____

_____

What do you know already? What do you want to know? What did you learn?

L A T I N

Copy your Latin memory work and try to write
last week's information from memory.

T H I S   W E E K

L A S T   W E E K

ENGLISH

Write in your weekly memory work for English.
Also, copy any advanced English memory work
if it applies to you. Below, write some sentences
that represent the memory work for the week.

Memory Work:

Write a sentence or short story that includes
some of the memory work as an example.
Or, diagram a sentence or two.

JOURNAL

Week 24

"ANXIETY DOES NOT EMPTY TOMORROW OF ITS SORROWS, BUT ONLY EMPTIES TODAY OF ITS STRENGTH." - CHARLES SPURGEON

WEEK TWENTY-FOUR

WRITE IN A GENERAL OVERVIEW OF YOUR WEEKLY MEMORY WORK TO GIVE
YOURSELF A WEEKLY AT-A-GLANCE OF YOUR WEEK AHEAD.

HISTORY
TIMELINE
GEOGRAPHY

ENGLISH

SCIENCE

BIBLE

MATH

LATIN

OTHER

HISTORY

Write your history memory work here 1-3 times.
Below, draw or paste a picture of this event.

_____

_____

_____

_____

_____

_____

_____

_____

GEOGRAPHY

WEEKLY TIMELINE

Label the year(s) and write the event in order from earliest (top) to latest (bottom). Draw a picture or paste a picture if you prefer to to it that way.

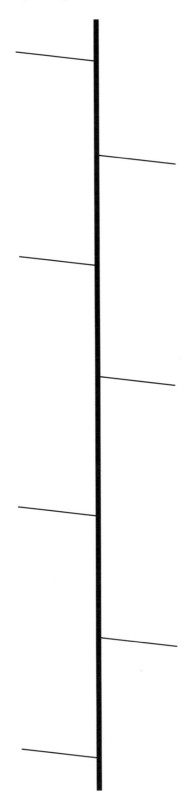

M A T H

Copy your math memory work here:

Make your own math problems and solve them:

Make your own number math maze, game, or
simply copy the memory work again:

B I B L E

Copy your selected weekly Bible verse(s), hymn,
etc. below. Answer the questions below.

_____

_____

_____

_____

_____

_____

_____

What did you learn about in this passage?

Write a prayer with some of these words in it.

SCIENCE

Write your science memory work in the lines below. Answer the questions below and/or draw your own picture and label it using the memory work.

_____

_____

_____

_____

_____

_____

What do you know already? What do you want to know? What did you learn?

L A T I N

Copy your Latin memory work and try to write
last week's information from memory.

T H I S   W E E K

L A S T   W E E K

ENGLISH

Write in your weekly memory work for English.
Also, copy any advanced English memory work
if it applies to you. Below, write some sentences
that represent the memory work for the week.

Memory Work:

Write a sentence or short story that includes
some of the memory work as an example.
Or, diagram a sentence or two.

JOURNAL

HERITAGE

Week 25

"FAITH DOES NOT ELIMINATE QUESTIONS. BUT FAITH KNOWS WHERE TO TAKE THEM." - ELISABETH ELLIOT

WEEK TWENTY-FIVE

WRITE IN A GENERAL OVERVIEW OF YOUR WEEKLY MEMORY WORK TO GIVE
YOURSELF A WEEKLY AT-A-GLANCE OF YOUR WEEK AHEAD.

HISTORY
TIMELINE
GEOGRAPHY

ENGLISH

SCIENCE

BIBLE

MATH

LATIN

OTHER

HISTORY

Write your history memory work here 1-3 times.
Below, draw or paste a picture of this event.

_____

_____

_____

_____

_____

_____

_____

_____

GEOGRAPHY

WEEKLY TIMELINE

Label the year(s) and write the event in order from earliest (top) to latest (bottom). Draw a picture or paste a picture if you prefer to to it that way.

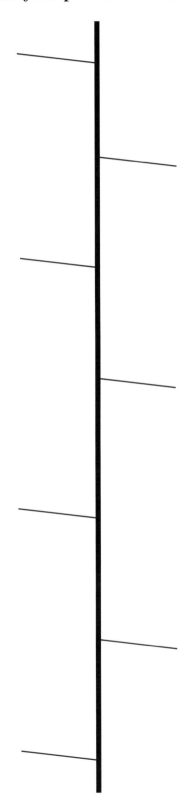

M A T H

Copy your math memory work here:

Make your own math problems and solve them:

Make your own number math maze, game, or
simply copy the memory work again:

BIBLE

Copy your selected weekly Bible verse(s), hymn, etc. below. Answer the questions below.

_____

_____

_____

_____

_____

_____

What did you learn about in this passage?

Write a prayer with some of these words in it.

SCIENCE

Write your science memory work in the lines below. Answer the questions below and/or draw your own picture and label it using the memory work.

_____

_____

_____

_____

_____

_____

What do you know already? What do you want to know? What did you learn?

L A T I N

Copy your Latin memory work and try to write
last week's information from memory.

T H I S   W E E K

L A S T   W E E K

ENGLISH

Write in your weekly memory work for English.
Also, copy any advanced English memory work
if it applies to you. Below, write some sentences
that represent the memory work for the week.

Memory Work:

~~~~~~

Write a sentence or short story that includes
some of the memory work as an example.
Or, diagram a sentence or two.

JOURNAL

HERİTAGE

Week 26

"COURAGE IS CONTAGIOUS. WHEN A BRAVE MAN TAKES A STAND, THE SPINES OF OTHERS ARE OFTEN STIFFENED." - BILLY GRAHAM

WEEK TWENTY-SIX

WRITE IN A GENERAL OVERVIEW OF YOUR WEEKLY MEMORY WORK TO GIVE
YOURSELF A WEEKLY AT-A-GLANCE OF YOUR WEEK AHEAD.

**HISTORY
TIMELINE
GEOGRAPHY**

ENGLISH

SCIENCE

BIBLE

MATH

LATIN

OTHER

HISTORY

Write your history memory work here 1-3 times. Below, draw or paste a picture of this event.

GEOGRAPHY

WEEKLY TIMELINE

Label the year(s) and write the event in order from earliest (top) to latest (bottom). Draw a picture or paste a picture if you prefer to to it that way.

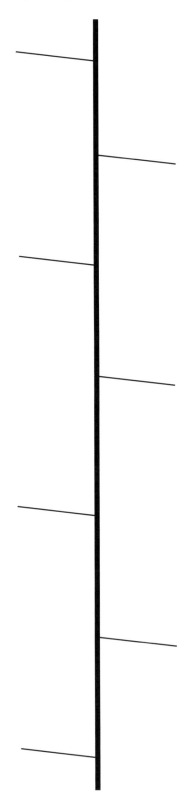

MATH

Copy your math memory work here:

Make your own math problems and solve them:

Make your own number math maze, game, or
simply copy the memory work again:

BIBLE

Copy your selected weekly Bible verse(s), hymn, etc. below. Answer the questions below.

_____

_____

_____

_____

_____

_____

What did you learn about in this passage?

Write a prayer with some of these words in it.

SCIENCE

Write your science memory work in the lines below. Answer the questions below and/or draw your own picture and label it using the memory work.

_____

_____

_____

_____

_____

_____

What do you know already? What do you want to know? What did you learn?

L A T I N

Copy your Latin memory work and try to write
last week's information from memory.

T H I S   W E E K

L A S T   W E E K

ENGLISH

Write in your weekly memory work for English.
Also, copy any advanced English memory work
if it applies to you. Below, write some sentences
that represent the memory work for the week.

Memory Work:

Write a sentence or short story that includes
some of the memory work as an example.
Or, diagram a sentence or two.

JOURNAL

"DO NOT GIVE WAY TO LOWNESS WHILE YOU ARE YOUNG. RISE UP ON THE STRENGTH OF GOD AND RESOLVE TO CONQUER."
– CATHERINE BOOTH

WEEK TWENTY-SEVEN

WRITE IN A GENERAL OVERVIEW OF YOUR WEEKLY MEMORY WORK TO GIVE
YOURSELF A WEEKLY AT-A-GLANCE OF YOUR WEEK AHEAD.

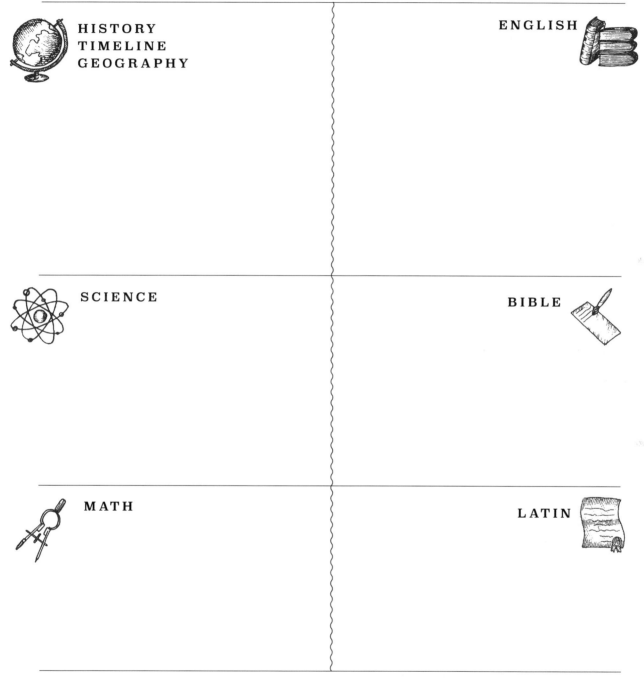

HISTORY
TIMELINE
GEOGRAPHY

ENGLISH

SCIENCE

BIBLE

MATH

LATIN

OTHER

HISTORY

Write your history memory work here 1-3 times.
Below, draw or paste a picture of this event.

GEOGRAPHY

WEEKLY TIMELINE

Label the year(s) and write the event in order from earliest (top) to latest (bottom). Draw a picture or paste a picture if you prefer to to it that way.

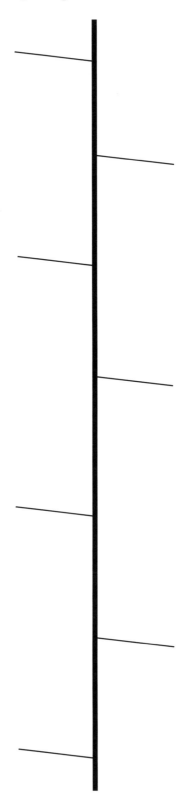

MATH

Copy your math memory work here:

Make your own math problems and solve them:

~~~~~~

Make your own number math maze, game, or
simply copy the memory work again:

BIBLE

Copy your selected weekly Bible verse(s), hymn,
etc. below. Answer the questions below.

_____

_____

_____

_____

_____

_____

_____

What did you learn about in this passage?

Write a prayer with some of these words in it.

SCIENCE

Write your science memory work in the lines below. Answer the questions below and/or draw your own picture and label it using the memory work.

_____

_____

_____

_____

_____

_____

What do you know already? What do you want to know? What did you learn?

L A T I N

Copy your Latin memory work and try to write
last week's information from memory.

T H I S   W E E K

L A S T   W E E K

ENGLISH

Write in your weekly memory work for English.
Also, copy any advanced English memory work
if it applies to you. Below, write some sentences
that represent the memory work for the week.

Memory Work:

Write a sentence or short story that includes
some of the memory work as an example.
Or, diagram a sentence or two.

JOURNAL

Week 28

"REFUSE TO BE AVERAGE. LET YOUR HEART SOAR AS HIGH AS IT WILL." - AW TOZER

WEEK TWENTY-EIGHT

WRITE IN A GENERAL OVERVIEW OF YOUR WEEKLY MEMORY WORK TO GIVE
YOURSELF A WEEKLY AT-A-GLANCE OF YOUR WEEK AHEAD.

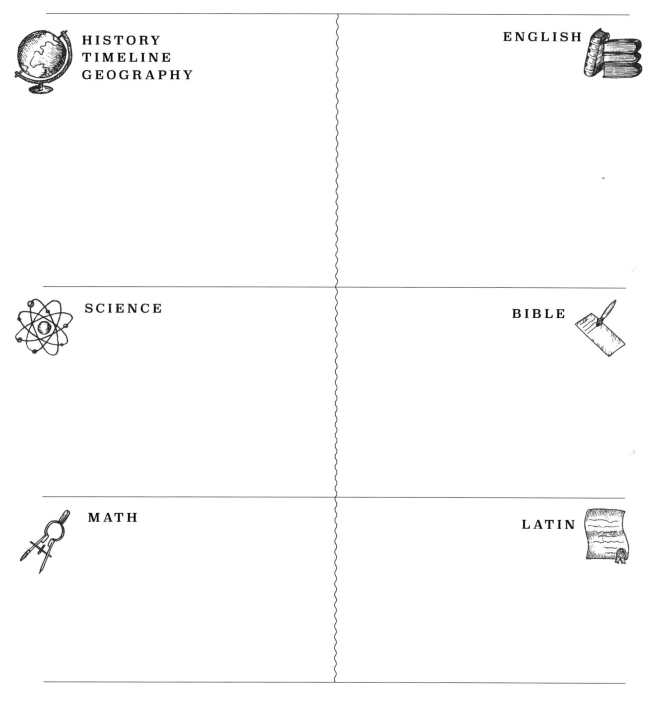

HISTORY
TIMELINE
GEOGRAPHY

ENGLISH

SCIENCE

BIBLE

MATH

LATIN

OTHER

HISTORY

Write your history memory work here 1-3 times.
Below, draw or paste a picture of this event.

_____

_____

_____

_____

_____

_____

_____

_____

GEOGRAPHY

WEEKLY TIMELINE

Label the year(s) and write the event in order from earliest (top) to latest (bottom). Draw a picture or paste a picture if you prefer to to it that way.

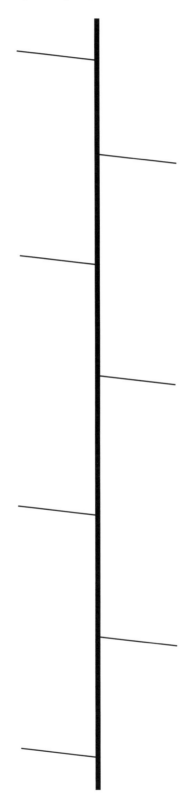

MATH

Copy your math memory work here:

Make your own math problems and solve them:

Make your own number math maze, game, or
simply copy the memory work again:

BIBLE

Copy your selected weekly Bible verse(s), hymn, etc. below. Answer the questions below.

_____

_____

_____

_____

_____

_____

_____

What did you learn about in this passage?

Write a prayer with some of these words in it.

SCIENCE

Write your science memory work in the lines below. Answer the questions below and/or draw your own picture and label it using the memory work.

_____

_____

_____

_____

_____

_____

What do you know already? What do you want to know? What did you learn?

L A T I N

Copy your Latin memory work and try to write
last week's information from memory.

T H I S   W E E K

L A S T   W E E K

ENGLISH

Write in your weekly memory work for English.
Also, copy any advanced English memory work
if it applies to you. Below, write some sentences
that represent the memory work for the week.

Memory Work:

Write a sentence or short story that includes
some of the memory work as an example.
Or, diagram a sentence or two.

REFERENCE

WORLD MAP

EASTERN HEMISPHERE

NORTH AMERICA

GREENLAND
(DENMARK)

CANADA

USA

MEXICO

HAWAII
(USA)

BAHAMAS

CUBA

DOMINICAN
REP.

HAITI

PUERTO
RICO

ANGUILLA (UK)

BELIZE

HONDURAS

JAMAICA

ST KITTS AND NEVIS

MONTSERRAT (UK)

ANTIGUA AND BARBUDA

GUADALUPE (FR)

DOMINICA

MARTINICA (FR)

GUATEMALA

EL SALVADOR

NICARAGUA

ST LUCIA

ST VINCENT & THE GRENADINES

BARBADOS

GRANADA

COSTA RICA

PANAMA

TRINIDAD AND TOBAGO

CENTRAL AMERICA, CARIBBEAN & PARTS OF SOUTH AMERICA

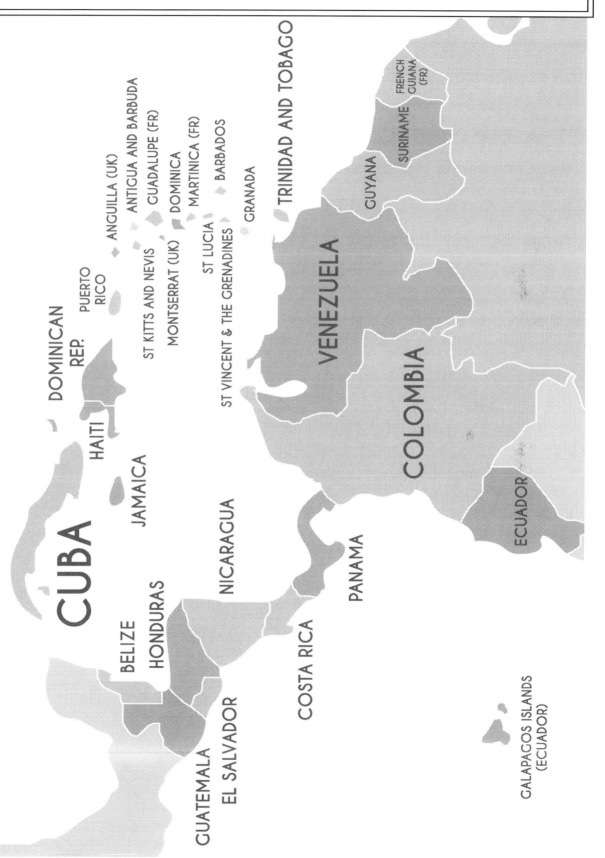

BAHAMAS

CUBA

DOMINICAN REP.

HAITI

JAMAICA

PUERTO RICO

ANGUILLA (UK)

ANTIGUA AND BARBUDA

GUADALUPE (FR)

ST KITTS AND NEVIS

MONTSERRAT (UK)

DOMINICA

MARTINICA (FR)

BARBADOS

ST LUCIA

ST VINCENT & THE GRENADINES

GRANADA

TRINIDAD AND TOBAGO

FRENCH GUIANA (FR)

SURINAME

GUYANA

VENEZUELA

COLOMBIA

ECUADOR

BELIZE

HONDURAS

NICARAGUA

GUATEMALA

EL SALVADOR

COSTA RICA

PANAMA

GALAPAGOS ISLANDS (ECUADOR)

USA MAP

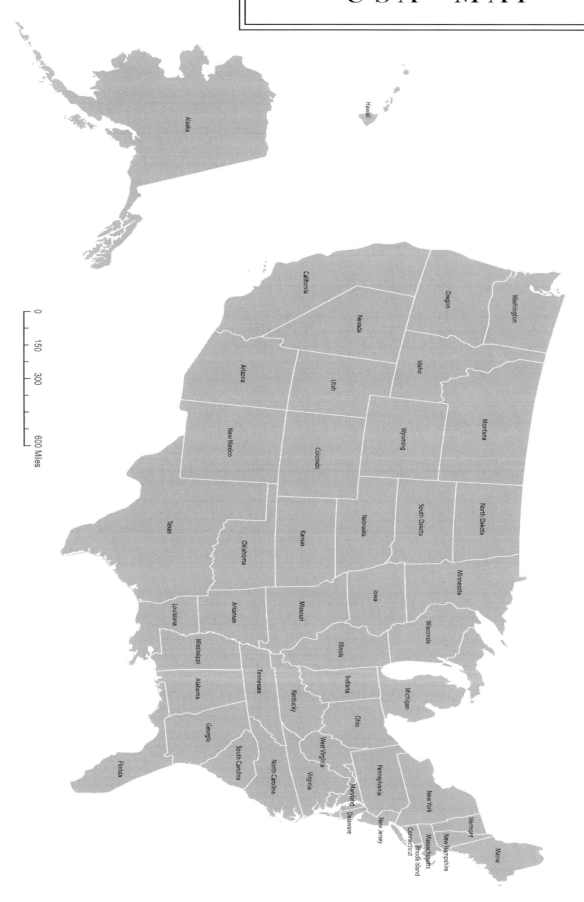

Alabama AL	New Mexico NM
Alaska AK	New York NY
Arizona AZ	North Carolina NC
Arkansas AR	North Dakota ND
California CA	Ohio OH
Colorado CO	Oklahoma OK
Connecticut CT	Oregon OR
Delaware DE	Pennsylvania PA
Florida FL	Rhode Island RI
Georgia GA	South Carolina SC
Hawaii HI	South Dakota SD
Idaho ID	Tennessee TN
Illinois IL	Texas TX
Indiana IN	Utah UT
Iowa IA	Vermont VT
Kansas KS	Virginia VA
Kentucky KY	Washington WA
Louisiana LA	West Virginia WV
Maine ME	Wisconsin WI
Maryland MD	Wyoming WY
Massachusetts MA	
Michigan MI	District of Columbia DC
Minnesota MN	Marshall Islands MH
Mississippi MS	
Missouri MO	Armed Forces Africa AE
Montana MT	Armed Forces Americas AA
Nebraska NE	Armed Forces Canada AE
Nevada NV	Armed Forces Europe AE
New Hampshire NH	Armed Forces Middle East AE
New Jersey NJ	Armed Forces Pacific AP

SOUTH AMERICA

VENEZUELA

GUYANA

COLOMBIA

SURINAME

FRENCH
GUIANA
(FR)

GALAPAGOS ISLANDS
(ECUADOR)

ECUADOR

BRAZIL

PERU

BOLIVIA

PARAGUAY

EASTER ISLAND
(CHILE)

CHILE

URUGUAY

ARGENTINA

FALKLAND ISLANDS
(UK)

SOUTH GEORGIAN ISLANDS
(UK)

OCEANA

SAMOA

FIJI

VANUATU

NEW CALEDONIA

SOLOMON ISLANDS

PAPUA NEW GUINEA

NEW ZEALAND

AUSTRALIA

EUROPE

ICELAND

FAROE
ISLANDS

NORWAY

FINLAND

SWEDEN

ESTONIA

DENMARK

LATVIA

LITHUANIA

RUSSIA

IRELAND

THE
NETHERLANDS

UK

BELARUS

POLAND

GERMANY

BELGIUM

UKRAINE

LUX.

CZECH REP.

SLOVAKIA

FRANCE

AUSTRIA

HUNGARY

MOLDOVA

SWITZ.

SLOV.

ROMANIA

ITALY

CROATIA

BOSNIA

SERBIA

MONACO

MONT.

KOS.

BULGARIA

MACED.

SPAIN

ALB.

PORTUGAL

MALTA

GREECE

EUROPE CLOSE-UP

AFRICA

TUNISIA
MADEIRA
(PORTUGAL)
MOROCCO
CANARY ISLANDS
(SPAIN)
ALGERIA
LIBYA
EGYPT
WESTERN
SAHARA
MAURITANIA
MALI
NIGER
SUDAN
ERITREA
CHAD
CAPE VERDE
SENEGAL
DJIBOUTI
GAMBIA
BURKINA
FASO
SOMALIA
GUINEA-
BISSAU
GUINEA
BENIN
NIGERIA
SOUTH
SUDAN
ETHIOPIA
SIERRA
LEONE
IVORY
COAST
CENTRAL AFRICAN
REPUBLIC
GHANA
LIBERIA
TOGO
CAMEROON
UGANDA
KENYA
EQUATORIAL
GUINEA
SAO TOME
& PRINCIPE
GABON
CONGO
(DEMOCRATIC
REPUBLIC)
RWANDA
BURUNDI
SEYCHELLES
CONGO
TANZANIA
COMOROS
MALAWI
MOZAMBIQUE
ANGOLA
ZAMBIA
MAURICIO
NAMIBIA
ZIMBABWE
REUNION
BOTSWANA
MADAGASCAR
SWAZILAND
LESOTHO
SOUTH
AFRICA

AFRICA CLOSE-UPS

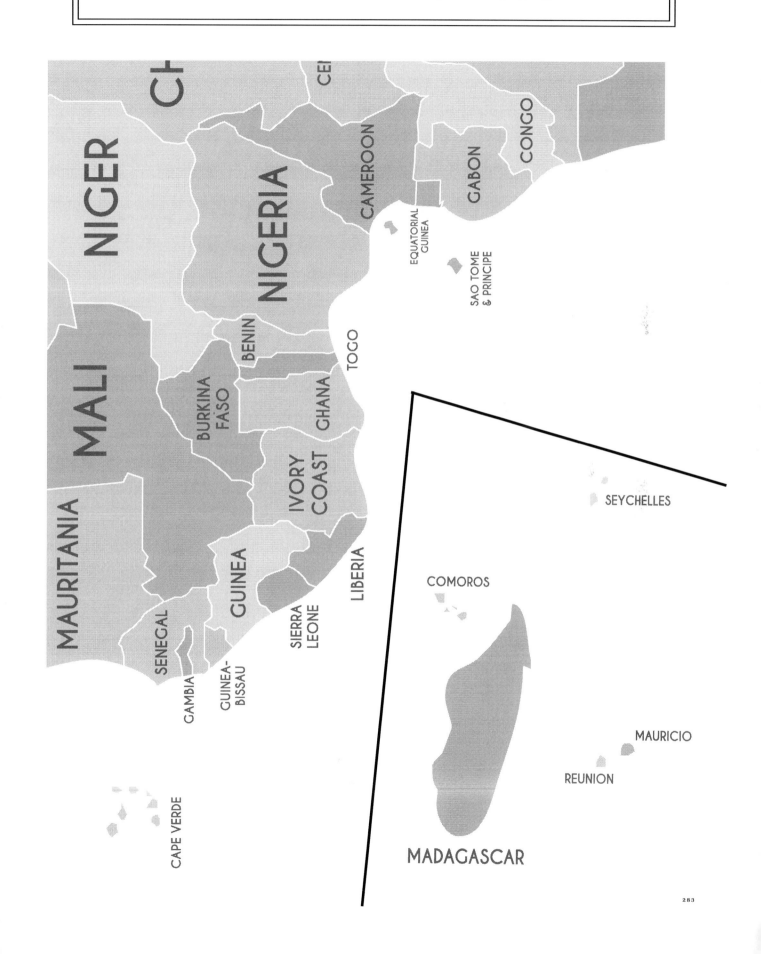

NIGER

CH

NIGERIA

MALI

MAURITANIA

CAMEROON

CENTR

CONGO

GABON

EQUATORIAL GUINEA

SAO TOME & PRINCIPE

BENIN

BURKINA FASO

GHANA

IVORY COAST

TOGO

GUINEA

LIBERIA

SIERRA LEONE

SENEGAL

GAMBIA

GUINEA-BISSAU

CAPE VERDE

SEYCHELLES

COMOROS

MAURICIO

REUNION

MADAGASCAR

ASIA

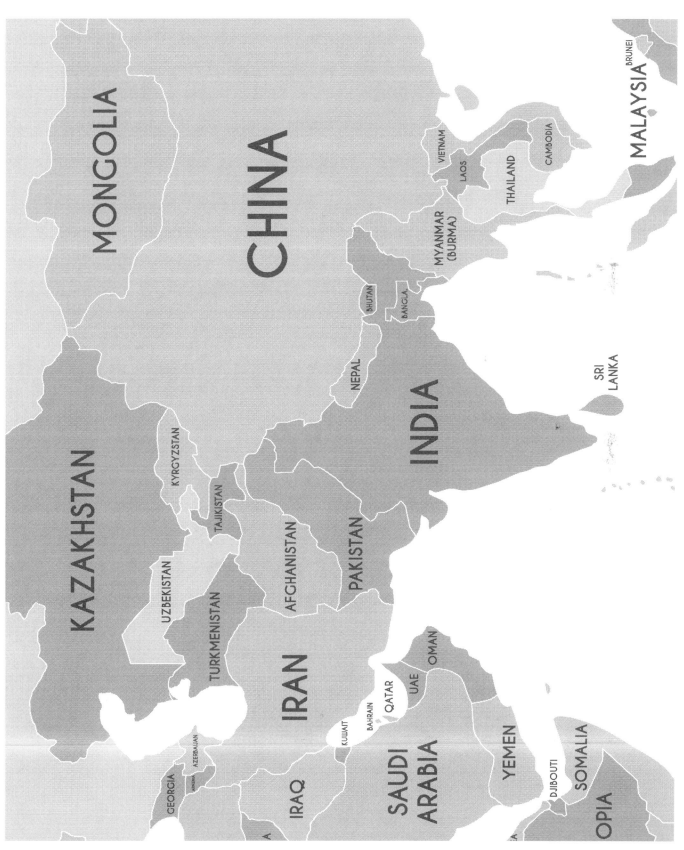

PERIODIC TABLE

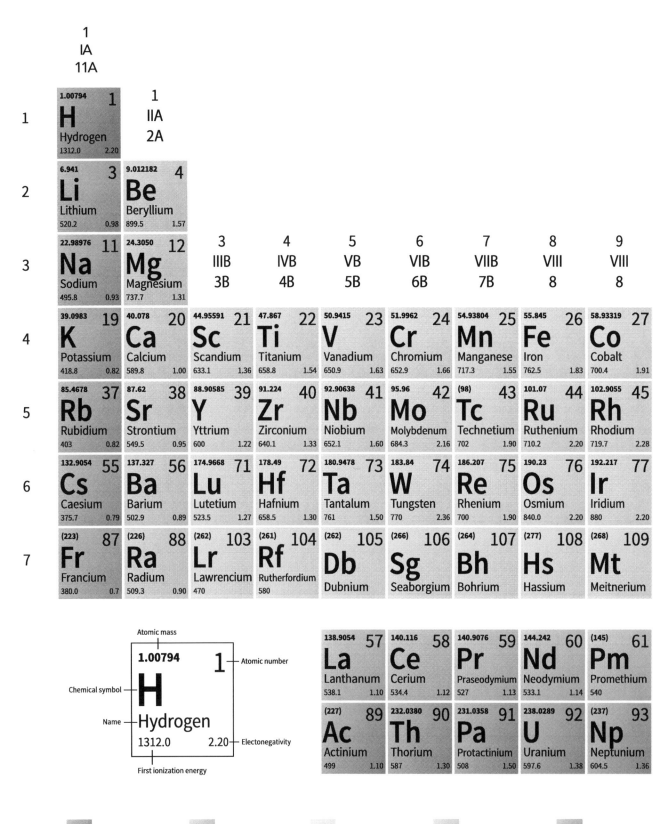

	1 IA 11A									
1	**1.00794** 1 **H** Hydrogen 1312.0 2.20	1 IIA 2A								
2	**6.941** 3 **Li** Lithium 520.2 0.98	**9.012182** 4 **Be** Beryllium 899.5 1.57								
3	**22.98976** 11 **Na** Sodium 495.8 0.93	**24.3050** 12 **Mg** Magnesium 737.7 1.31	3 IIIB 3B	4 IVB 4B	5 VB 5B	6 VIB 6B	7 VIIB 7B	8 VIII 8	9 VIII 8	

4	**39.0983** 19 **K** Potassium 418.8 0.82	**40.078** 20 **Ca** Calcium 589.8 1.00	**44.95591** 21 **Sc** Scandium 633.1 1.36	**47.867** 22 **Ti** Titanium 658.8 1.54	**50.9415** 23 **V** Vanadium 650.9 1.63	**51.9962** 24 **Cr** Chromium 652.9 1.66	**54.93804** 25 **Mn** Manganese 717.3 1.55	**55.845** 26 **Fe** Iron 762.5 1.83	**58.93319** 27 **Co** Cobalt 700.4 1.91
5	**85.4678** 37 **Rb** Rubidium 403 0.82	**87.62** 38 **Sr** Strontium 549.5 0.95	**88.90585** 39 **Y** Yttrium 600 1.22	**91.224** 40 **Zr** Zirconium 640.1 1.33	**92.90638** 41 **Nb** Niobium 652.1 1.60	**95.96** 42 **Mo** Molybdenum 684.3 2.16	**(98)** 43 **Tc** Technetium 702 1.90	**101.07** 44 **Ru** Ruthenium 710.2 2.20	**102.9055** 45 **Rh** Rhodium 719.7 2.28
6	**132.9054** 55 **Cs** Caesium 375.7 0.79	**137.327** 56 **Ba** Barium 502.9 0.89	**174.9668** 71 **Lu** Lutetium 523.5 1.27	**178.49** 72 **Hf** Hafnium 658.5 1.30	**180.9478** 73 **Ta** Tantalum 761 1.50	**183.84** 74 **W** Tungsten 770 2.36	**186.207** 75 **Re** Rhenium 700 1.90	**190.23** 76 **Os** Osmium 840.0 2.20	**192.217** 77 **Ir** Iridium 880 2.20
7	**(223)** 87 **Fr** Francium 380.0 0.7	**(226)** 88 **Ra** Radium 509.3 0.90	**(262)** 103 **Lr** Lawrencium 470	**(261)** 104 **Rf** Rutherfordium 580	**(262)** 105 **Db** Dubnium	**(266)** 106 **Sg** Seaborgium	**(264)** 107 **Bh** Bohrium	**(277)** 108 **Hs** Hassium	**(268)** 109 **Mt** Meitnerium

Legend box:
Atomic mass — **1.00794**
Atomic number — 1
Chemical symbol — **H**
Name — Hydrogen
First ionization energy — 1312.0
Electonegativity — 2.20

138.9054 57 **La** Lanthanum 538.1 1.10	**140.116** 58 **Ce** Cerium 534.4 1.12	**140.9076** 59 **Pr** Praseodymium 527 1.13	**144.242** 60 **Nd** Neodymium 533.1 1.14	**(145)** 61 **Pm** Promethium 540
(227) 89 **Ac** Actinium 499 1.10	**232.0380** 90 **Th** Thorium 587 1.30	**231.0358** 91 **Pa** Protactinium 508 1.50	**238.0289** 92 **U** Uranium 597.6 1.38	**(237)** 93 **Np** Neptunium 604.5 1.36

Alkali metals Alkaline metals Other metals Transition metals Lanthanoids

						18
						VIIIA
						8A

13	14	15	16	17	4.002602 **He** 2
IIIA	IVA	VA	VIA	VIIA	Helium
3A	4A	5A	6A	7A	2372.3

			10.811 **B** 5	12.0107 **C** 6	14.0067 **N** 7	15.9994 **O** 8	18.998403 **F** 9	20.1797 **Ne** 10
			Boron	Carbon	Nitrogen	Oxygen	Fluorine	Neon
			800.6 2.04	1086.5 2.55	1402.3 3.04	1313.9 3.44	1681 3.98	2080.7

10	11	12	26.98153 **Al** 13	28.0855 **Si** 14	30.97696 **P** 15	32.065 **S** 16	35.453 **Cl** 17	39.948 **Ar** 18
VIII	IB	IIB	Aluminium	Silicon	Phosphorus	Sulfur	Chlorine	Iron
8	1B	2B	577.5 1.61	786.5 1.90	1011.8 2.19	999.6 2.58	1251.2 3.16	1520.6

58.6934 **Ni** 28	63.546 **Cu** 29	65.38 **Zn** 30	69.723 **Ga** 31	72.64 **Ge** 32	74.92160 **As** 33	78.96 **Se** 34	79.904 **Br** 35	83.798 **Kr** 36
Nickel	Copper	Zinc	Gallium	Germanium	Arsenic	Selenium	Bromine	Krypton
737.1 1.88	745.5 1.90	906.4 1.65	578.8 1.81	762 2.01	947 2.18	941 2.55	1139.9 2.96	1350.8

106.42 **Pd** 46	107.8682 **Ag** 47	112.441 **Cd** 48	114.818 **In** 49	118.710 **Sn** 50	121.760 **Sb** 51	127.60 **Te** 52	126.9044 **I** 53	131.293 **Xe** 54
Palladium	Silver	Cadmium	Indium	Tin	Antimony	Tellurium	Iodine	Xenon
804.4 2.20	731 1.93	867.8 1.69	558.3 1.78	708.6 1.96	834 2.05	869.3 2.10	1008.4 2.66	1170.4 2.60

195.084 **Pt** 78	196.9665 **Au** 79	200.59 **Hg** 80	204.3833 **Tl** 81	207.2 **Pb** 82	208.9804 **Bi** 83	(210) **Po** 84	(210) **At** 85	(220) **Rn** 86
Platinum	Gold	Mercury	Thallium	Lead	Bismuth	Polonium	Astatine	Radon
870 2.28	890.1 2.54	1007.1 2.00	589.4 1.62	715.6 2.33	703 2.02	812.1 2.00	890 2.20	1037

(271) **Ds** 110	(272) **Rg** 111	(285) **Cn** 112	(284) **Uut** 113	(289) **Fl** 114	(228) **Uup** 115	(292) **Lv** 116	**Uus** 117	(294) **Uuo** 118
Darmstadium	Roentgenium	Copernicium	Ununtrium	Flerovium	Ununpentium	Livermorium	Ununseptium	Ununoctium

150.36 **Sm** 62	151.964 **Eu** 63	157.25 **Gd** 64	158.9253 **Tb** 65	162.500 **Dy** 66	164.9303 **Ho** 67	167.259 **Er** 68	168.9342 **Tm** 69	173.054 **Yb** 70
Samarium	Europium	Gadolinium	Terbium	Dysprosium	Holmium	Erbium	Thulium	Ytterbium
544.5 1.17	547.1	593.4 1.20	565.8	573 1.22	581 1.23	589.3 1.24	596.7 1.25	603.4

(244) **Pu** 94	(243) **Am** 95	(247) **Cm** 96	(247) **Bk** 97	(251) **Cf** 98	(252) **Es** 99	(257) **Fm** 100	(258) **Md** 101	(259) **No** 102
Plutonium	Americium	Curium	Berkelium	Californium	Einsteinium	Fermium	Mendelevium	Nobelium
584.7 1.28	578 1.30	581 1.30	601 1.30	608 1.30	619 1.30	627 1.30	635 1.30	642 1.30

Actinoids   Metalloids   Nonmetals   Halogens   Noble gases

THE SOLAR SYSTEM

Label the planets with the key
below and write facts about
them on the right.

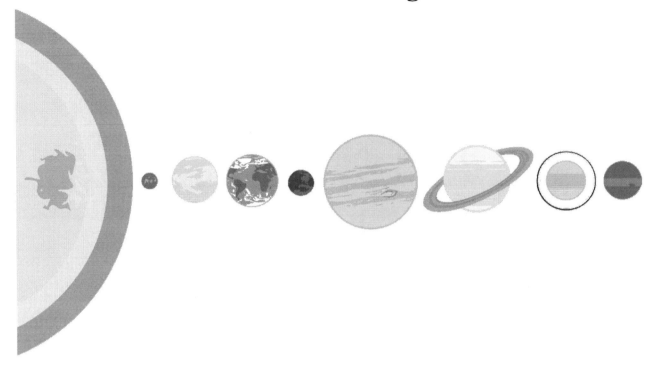

SUN

MERCURY

VENUS

EARTH

MARS

JUPITER

SATURN

URANUS

NEPTUNE

NEW MOON

 WAXING (GROWING) CRESCENT

 FIRST QUARTER

 WAXING GIBBOUS

 FULL MOON

 WANING (DECREASING) CRESCENT

 SECOND QUARTER

 WANING GIBBOUS

BOTANY LABELS

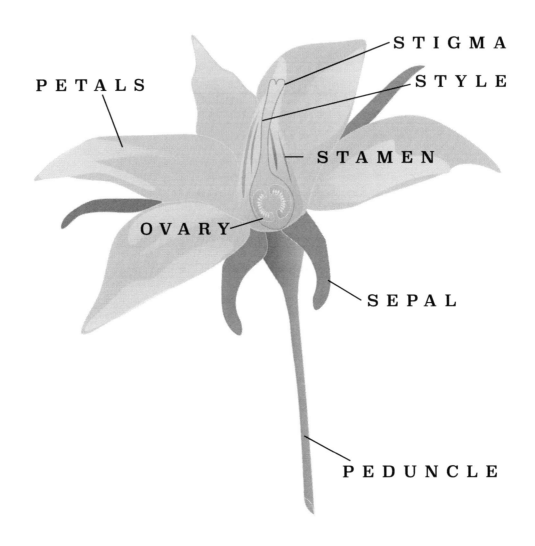

STIGMA

STYLE

PETALS

STAMEN

OVARY

SEPAL

PEDUNCLE

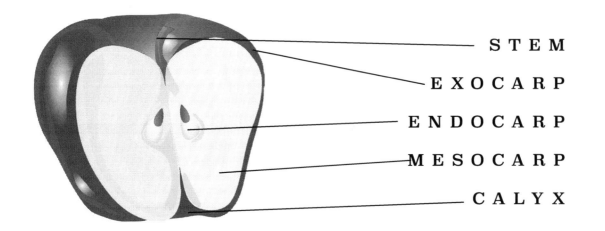

STEM

EXOCARP

ENDOCARP

MESOCARP

CALYX

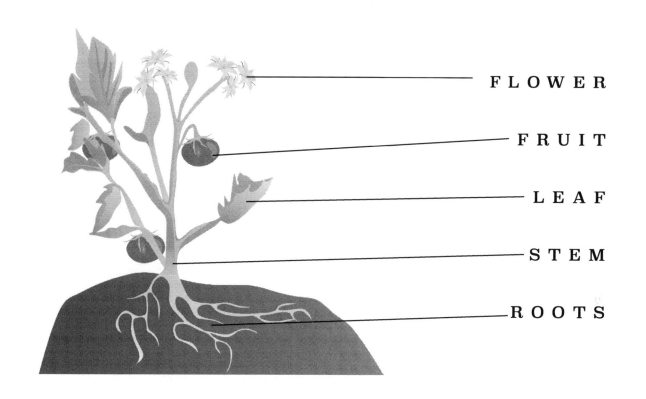

FLOWER

FRUIT

LEAF

STEM

ROOTS

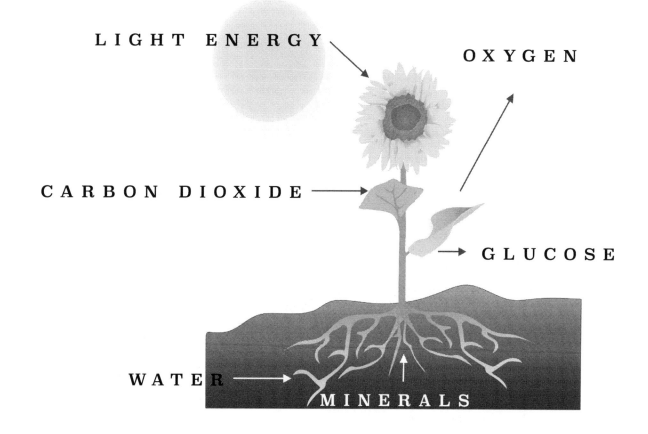

LIGHT ENERGY

OXYGEN

CARBON DIOXIDE

GLUCOSE

WATER

MINERALS

EARTH & MINERALS

MOHS SCALE OF HARDNESS

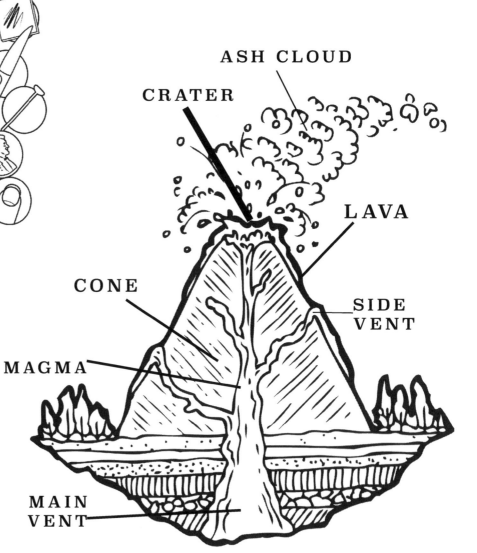

(10) diamond

(9) corundum

(8) topaz

(7) quartz

streak plate
(6) orthoclase

glass
knife
(5) apatite

wire nail
(4) fluorite

copper penny
(3) calcite

fingernail
(2) gypsum

(1) talc

ASH CLOUD

CRATER

LAVA

CONE

SIDE VENT

MAGMA

MAIN VENT

Continental Margin and Abyssal Plain

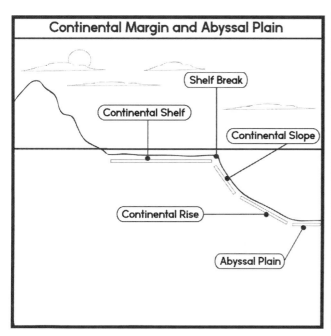

Shelf Break

Continental Shelf

Continental Slope

Continental Rise

Abyssal Plain

Ocean Floor Features

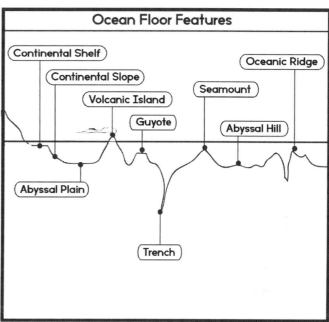

Continental Shelf

Continental Slope

Volcanic Island

Guyote

Seamount

Oceanic Ridge

Abyssal Hill

Abyssal Plain

Trench

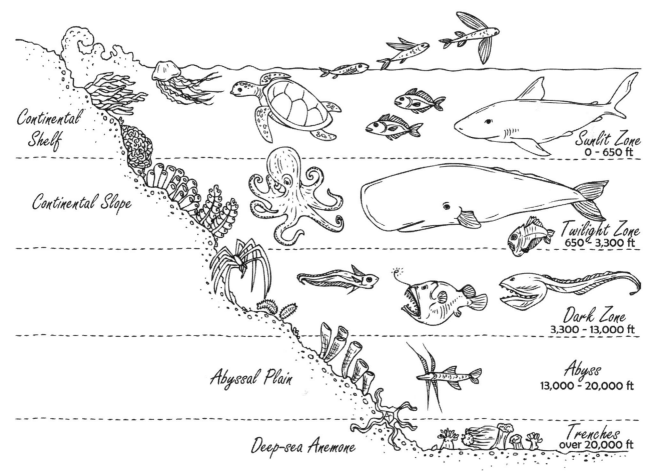

Continental Shelf

Continental Slope

Abyssal Plain

Deep-sea Anemone

Sunlit Zone
0 - 650 ft

Twilight Zone
650 - 3,300 ft

Dark Zone
3,300 - 13,000 ft

Abyss
13,000 - 20,000 ft

Trenches
over 20,000 ft

Cirrus
High- Level Clouds
over 20,000 ft.

Cumulonimbus
1,600 to 39,000 ft.

Cumulus
2,000 to 4,000 ft.

Altocumulus
Mid- Level Clouds
6,500 to 20,000 ft.

Altostratus

Stratus

Stratocumulus
Low- Level Clouds
surface to 6,500 ft.

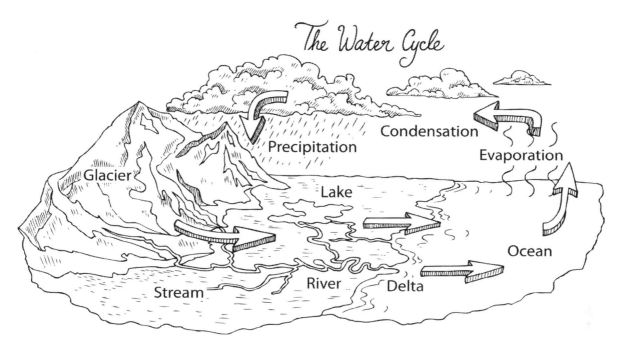

The Water Cycle

THUNDERSTORMS

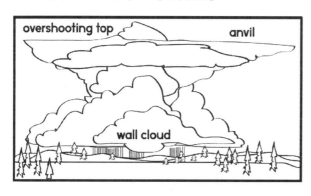

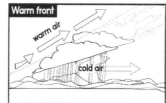

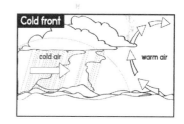

TORNADOS

HURRICANES

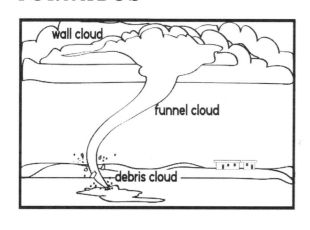

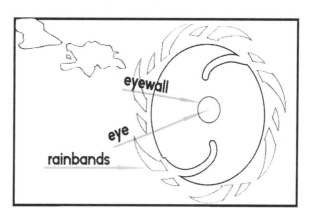

ANATOMY

Circulatory system

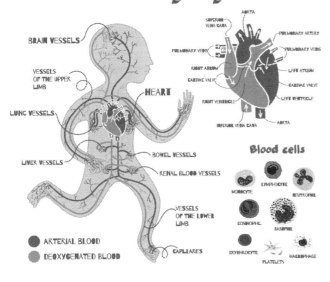

BRAIN VESSELS

VESSELS OF THE UPPER LIMB

LUNG VESSELS

LIVER VESSELS

HEART

BOWEL VESSELS

RENAL BLOOD VESSELS

VESSELS OF THE LOWER LIMB

CAPILLARIES

ARTERIAL BLOOD
DEOXYGENATED BLOOD

SUPERIOR VENA CAVA
AORTA
PULMONARY ARTERY
PULMONARY VEINS
PULMONARY VEINS
RIGHT ATRIUM
LEFT ATRIUM
CARDIAC VALVE
CARDIAC VALVE
RIGHT VENTRICLE
LEFT VENTRICLE
INFERIOR VENA CAVA
AORTA

Blood cells

MONOCYTE
LYMPHOCYTE
NEUTROPHIL
EOSINOPHIL
BASOPHIL
ERYTHROCYTE
MACROPHAGE
PLATELETS

Digestive system

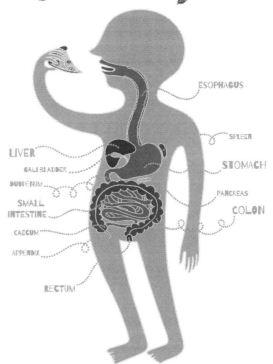

ESOPHAGUS

LIVER
GALLBLADDER
DUODENUM
SMALL INTESTINE
CAECUM
APPENDIX
RECTUM

SPLEEN
STOMACH
PANCREAS
COLON

Nervous system

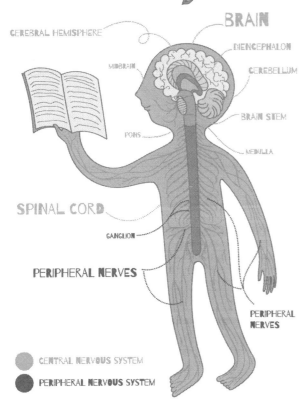

CEREBRAL HEMISPHERE
BRAIN
DIENCEPHALON
MIDBRAIN
CEREBELLUM
BRAIN STEM
PONS
MEDULLA
SPINAL CORD
GANGLION
PERIPHERAL NERVES
PERIPHERAL NERVES

CENTRAL NERVOUS SYSTEM
PERIPHERAL NERVOUS SYSTEM

Respiratory system

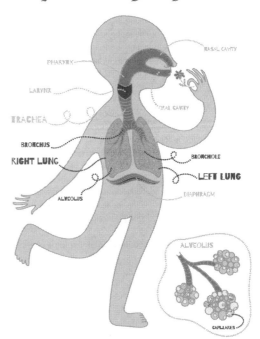

PHARYNX
LARYNX
TRACHEA
BRONCHUS
RIGHT LUNG
ALVEOLUS

NASAL CAVITY
ORAL CAVITY
BRONCHIOLE
LEFT LUNG
DIAPHRAGM

ALVEOLUS
CAPILLARIES

Muscular system

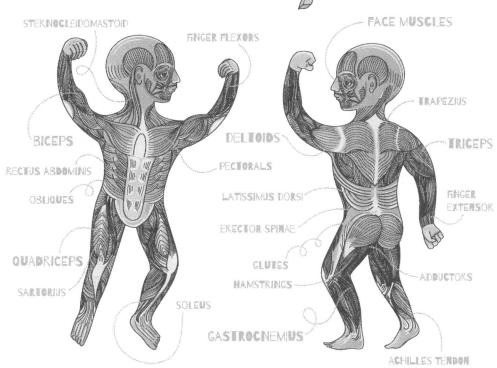

STERNOCLEIDOMASTOID
FINGER FLEXORS
FACE MUSCLES
TRAPEZIUS
BICEPS
DELTOIDS
TRICEPS
RECTUS ABDOMINIS
PECTORALS
OBLIQUES
LATISSIMUS DORSI
FINGER EXTENSOR
ERECTOR SPINAE
QUADRICEPS
GLUTES
SARTORIUS
HAMSTRINGS
ADDUCTORS
SOLEUS
GASTROCNEMIUS
ACHILLES TENDON

Skeletal system

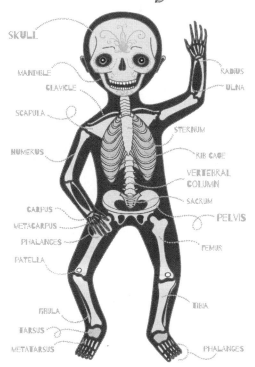

SKULL
MANDIBLE
RADIUS
CLAVICLE
ULNA
SCAPULA
STERNUM
HUMERUS
RIB CAGE
VERTEBRAL COLUMN
SACRUM
CARPUS
PELVIS
METACARPUS
PHALANGES
FEMUR
PATELLA
FIBULA
TIBIA
TARSUS
METATARSUS
PHALANGES

Endocrine system

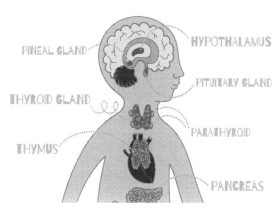

PINEAL GLAND
HYPOTHALAMUS
THYROID GLAND
PITUITARY GLAND
PARATHYROID
THYMUS
PANCREAS

1. EYE CONTACT

2. POSTURE

3. VOLUME

4. FILLER WORDS

5. ARTICULATION

6. TENOR

7. EMOTION/CONNECTION

THE PREAMBLE TO THE BILL OF RIGHTS

Congress of the United States
begun and held at the City of New-York, on
Wednesday the fourth of March, one thousand seven hundred and eighty
nine.

THE Conventions of a number of the States, having at the time of their
adopting the Constitution, expressed a desire, in order to prevent mis-
construction or abuse of its powers, that further declaratory and restric-
tive clauses should be added: And as extending the ground of public
confidence in the Government, will best ensure the beneficent ends of its
institution.

RESOLVED by the Senate and House of Representatives of the United
States of America, in Congress assembled, two thirds of both Houses con-
curring, that the following Articles be proposed to the Legislatures of the
several States, as amendments to the Constitution of the United States,
all, or any of which Articles, when ratified by three fourths of the said
Legislatures, to be valid to all intents and purposes, as part of the said
Constitution; viz.

ARTICLES in addition to, and Amendment of the Constitution of the United States of America, proposed by Congress, and ratified by the Legislatures of the several States, pursuant to the fifth Article of the original
Constitution.

Note: The following text is a transcription of the first ten amendments to
the Constitution in their original form. These amendments were ratified
December 15, 1791, and form what is known as the "Bill of Rights."

Amendment I

Congress shall make no law respecting an establishment of religion, or
prohibiting the free exercise thereof; or abridging the freedom of speech,
or of the press; or the right of the people peaceably to assemble, and to
petition the Government for a redress of grievances.

Amendment II

A well regulated Militia, being necessary to the security of a free State,
the right of the people to keep and bear Arms, shall not be infringed.

Amendment III

No Soldier shall, in time of peace be quartered in any house, without
the consent of the Owner, nor in time of war, but in a manner to be pre-
scribed by law.

Amendment IV

The right of the people to be secure in their persons, houses, papers, and effects, against unreasonable searches and seizures, shall not be violated, and no Warrants shall issue, but upon probable cause, supported by Oath or affirmation, and particularly describing the place to be searched, and the persons or things to be seized.

Amendment V

No person shall be held to answer for a capital, or otherwise infamous crime, unless on a presentment or indictment of a Grand Jury, except in cases arising in the land or naval forces, or in the Militia, when in actual service in time of War or public danger; nor shall any person be subject for the same offence to be twice put in jeopardy of life or limb; nor shall be compelled in any criminal case to be a witness against himself, nor be deprived of life, liberty, or property, without due process of law; nor shall private property be taken for public use, without just compensation.

Amendment VI

In all criminal prosecutions, the accused shall enjoy the right to a speedy and public trial, by an impartial jury of the State and district wherein the crime shall have been committed, which district shall have been previously ascertained by law, and to be informed of the nature and cause of the accusation; to be confronted with the witnesses against him; to have compulsory process for obtaining witnesses in his favor, and to have the Assistance of Counsel for his defence.

Amendment VII

In Suits at common law, where the value in controversy shall exceed twenty dollars, the right of trial by jury shall be preserved, and no fact tried by a jury, shall be otherwise re-examined in any Court of the United States, than according to the rules of the common law.

Amendment VIII

Excessive bail shall not be required, nor excessive fines imposed, nor cruel and unusual punishments inflicted.

Amendment IX

The enumeration in the Constitution, of certain rights, shall not be construed to deny or disparage others retained by the people.

Amendment X

The powers not delegated to the United States by the Constitution, nor prohibited by it to the States, are reserved to the States respectively, or to the people.

PREAMBLE OF THE CONSTITUTION OF THE UNITED STATES

We the People of the United States, in Order to form a more perfect Union, establish Justice, insure domestic Tranquility, provide for the common defence, promote the general Welfare, and secure the Blessings of Liberty to ourselves and our Posterity, do ordain and establish this Constitution for the United States of America.

PLEDGE OF ALLEGIANCES

TO THE BIBLE:

I pledge allegiance to the Bible, God's Holy Word, I will make it a lamp unto my feet and a light unto my path and will hide its words in my heart that I might not sin against God.

TO THE AMERICAN FLAG:

I pledge allegiance to the flag of the United States of America and to the Republic for which it stands, one Nation under God, indivisible, with liberty and justice for all.

EXCERPT FROM THE DECLARATION OF INDEPENDENCE

We hold these truths to be self-evident, that all men are created equal, that they are endowed by their Creator with certain unalienable Rights, that among these are Life, Liberty and the pursuit of Happiness. That to secure these rights, Governments are instituted among Men, deriving their just powers from the consent of the governed, That whenever any Form of Government becomes destructive of these ends, it is the Right of the People to alter or to abolish it, and to institute new Government, laying its foundation on such principles and organizing its powers in such form, as to them shall seem most likely to effect their Safety and Happiness.

THE TEN COMMANDMENTS

1. You shall have no other gods before me.
2. You shall not make yourself a carved image, or any likeness of anything that is in heaven above, or that is in the earth beneath, or that is in the water under the earth. You shall not bow down to them or serve them, for I the Lord your God are only worthy of worship, visiting the iniquity of the fathers on the children to the third and the fourth generation of those who hate me, but showing steadfast love to thousands of those who love me and keep my commandments.
3. You shall not take the name of the Lord your God in vain, for the Lord will not hold him guiltless who takes his name in vain.
4. Remember the Sabbath day, to keep it holy. Six days you shall labor, and do all your work, but the seventh day is a Sabbath to the Lord your God. On it you shall not do any work, you, or your son, or your daughter, or your servant, or your livestock, or the sojourner who is within your gates. For in six days the Lord made heaven and earth, the sea, and all that is in them, and rested on the seventh day. Therefore the Lord blessed the Sabbath day and made it holy.
5. Honor your father and your mother, that your days may be long in the land that the Lord your God is giving you.
6. You shall not murder.
7. You shall not commit adultery.
8. You shall not steal.
9. You shall not bear false witness against your neighbor.
10. You shall not covet your neighbor's house; you shall not covet your neighbor's wife, or his male servant, or his female servant, or his ox, or his donkey, or anything that is your neighbor's.